Sheri's writing is rich in meaningful metaphor which connects the listener with spirit and soul. Her songs' lyrics and rich images leave one feeling understood, and satisfied.
~ Dr. Jerry R. Wright, Jungian analyst

☙

Sheri's message is inspiring for those who are seeking their true journey and even those solidly on it. Her uplifting spirit and earnest music are scrumptious food for the soul.
~ Dale Harrison, former chair, Department of
Communication & Journalism, Auburn University

☙

Sheri Kling is a charismatic performer and presenter and her presentation on the archetypal hero and the creative writing process was well received. I really cannot say enough about Sheri. My students still sing "Train to Metaphor" anytime we speak of symbolism in class. They loved her visit and the assignment that followed. Sheri even inspired me to write and share my creative piece with my students. I highly recommend Sheri Kling as a guest speaker to any English or Humanities classroom. Her presentation is one students will remember for years.
~ Rebecca Perkins, English Teacher,
Alpharetta High School, Alpharetta, GA

☙

Our congregation enjoyed your music, especially the peaceful feeling you communicated. Even more, I appreciated your theology – a proclamation of grace. As you sang of rest and peace, so you created an atmosphere of sabbath and renewal. Your music gave witness to the loving kindness of our God. Thanks again for your good ministry. We are better because of it.
~ Rev. Rick Sebastian, Zion Lutheran, Guyton, GA

☙

What a treat to hear your music! It is rich and powerful, capable of moving people to action and tears. There were so many people who spoke to me of their appreciation for your music. Thank you for taking the time to share with us your multiple gifts. I heard great things about your workshop. It is wonderful to have you as a friend of Mary & Martha's Place. We look forward to future collaboration.
~ Rebecca Parker, Program Developer,
Mary & Martha's Place, Atlanta, GA

℘

What wonderful comments we received on both your musical/ vocal talent and the warm and touching message you delivered to us in our recent Sunday morning service. Even weeks later, I still am hearing kudos on bringing you to our people. I did good! And you should know that I personally enjoyed your inspirational style immensely. Your message fit in so well with what we teach at Unity and your songs did the same. I would heartily recommend you to any other Unity ministry! We appreciate your making it so easy for us to have you perform here. Your requirements were minimal and that made it smooth for our technicians and me in setting up.
~ Rev. Kent Lederer, Unity of Savannah, GA

℘

I wanted to thank you again for a moving, special evening; of feeling a part of your journey through your heartfelt songs--It was indeed special and a breath of the personal that is always more meaningful to me than the more usual lectures!
~ Kay Fedel, C.G. Jung Society of Sarasota, Sarasota, FL

℘

OTHER WORKS BY THE AUTHOR

MUSIC

Let It Unfold (2002)
Heartland (2005)
Passions & Prodigals (2005)

SHERI KLING

HeartSprings Books

Finding Home

Rural reflections on the journey to wholeness

To Pam + David.
I hope you enjoy
my stories of "home."

Sh... K...
3-26-2005

HeartSprings Books
HeartSprings Productions, LLC
P.O. Box 1804
Clarkesville, Georgia 30523
706-839-1333 · www.sherikling.com

First published by HeartSprings Books in
association with Gather Community Press   11/26/2008

ISBN: 978-1-9350-2805-5 (sc)

Printed in the United States of America
Boston, Massachusetts

This book is printed on acid-free paper.

Most of the included essays were first published in
The Northeast Georgian newspaper in 2007 and
2008. All rights retained by the author.

All photos © 2008 by Sheri Kling
except for back cover photo by Anne Parke
Anne Parke Photography, Marietta, GA
www.anneparkephotography.com

Text written by Henri Nouwen as quoted in the essay
"Finding Home" are from his book
"The Return of the Prodigal Son: A Story of Homecoming"
Image Books/Doubleday, 1994, 1992

With gratitude to God
for a journey that has been filled
with richness, depth and grace.
And for my dear friend Verna Brown
whose encouraging voice
has been a treasure to me.

Contents

Foreword

Home. It's something we leave early on, then yearn for the rest of our lives. And whether "home" is a compass-point place or a way of fully living in our own lives, our own bodies and our own spirits, finding where we "fit" is finding our true home.

This writing comes out of the Southern foothills of the Appalachian Mountains in northeast Georgia; from a place to which I retreated so I could better hear my own voice. I've spent nearly two years living in this rural mountain community and have tried in these essays to communicate what I have found here – and what I have found within me.

Ever since May of 2003 when I lost my last full-time day job in marketing for a software company, I'd been building my career as a performing singer-songwriter, guitarist, recording artist and keynote speaker. And like most artists, I've always had to supplement my creative work with something that will keep the bills paid. In trying to earn my living

1

after I moved from metropolitan Atlanta to Demorest, Georgia, I was writing press releases for the local technical college to promote workshops they offered to small businesses. I usually submitted those press releases to local newspapers in the seven county region served by the college. In Habersham County, my own place of residence, those submissions went to Rob Moore, editor of *The Northeast Georgian*. In one email, I casually remarked that "one of these days" I would submit an idea for a column.

He responded right away, asking me what I would write about. This was my answer:

Well, it might take a cup of coffee's worth of conversation to flesh out (as I've never pitched a column before), but everything I write musically draws from what I would call the journey toward passionate, authentic living.

In the PBS special and book "Joseph Campbell and The Power of Myth," Campbell said "People say that what we're all seeking is a meaning for life. I don't think that's what we're really seeking. I think that what we're seeking is an experience of being alive, so that our life experiences on the purely physical plane will have resonances within our own innermost being and reality, so that we actually feel the rapture of being alive."

I'm 46 years old, single, no children (not for lack of interest or looking!) and so my life has centered

*on the journey toward finding that experience
of rapture and then trying to communicate that
journey in some way. Psychologists call that journey
individuation, theologians call it wholeness. For
me, the universe is God's mouthpiece, and I look
for guidance everywhere—in nature, in dreams, in
conversations with friends, in wisdom stories from
all over. The latest step in that journey for me was
to unplug from everything I knew in Marietta (I
lived in the same condominium for 25 years and
went to the same church for just as long) and throw
myself at the mercy of the Universe, God, and the
angels because I wanted to live in this beautiful part
of Georgia, where the pastures and hawks and even
the siding of my old barn speak to me.*

*And I'm enthralled by the things I'm learning
by moving to a small town in the country – for
example, I had no idea that chickens had earlobes
and you could tell what color their eggs would be
by those earlobes.*

*So I would write a column based on those
observations and that journey.*

Unbelievably, Rob actually accepted these ideas
as reasonable in the context of a small, mostly-
conservative, mostly-Christian community with a
newspaper that is published twice per week, and
asked me to start submitting columns.

So, beginning in May of 2007 with my essay "Out of the Box," what began to flow from my mind and heart is what you will find in the pages of this book, presented in the order in which they were written. It has been a journey that I've thoroughly enjoyed. My hope is that you will find something of value here as you follow your own journey toward Home.

~ Sheri Kling, October, 2008

Companions

Out of the Box

Until this past December 15, I lived in a box with limited windows that was high above the ground. No, I'm not a former resident of one of the state's prisons, just of a condo in Marietta, Georgia. Maybe some would see that as a jail of sorts. For me, what felt most confined in that space was my soul.

Don't get me wrong, it had been a great place to live. The mortgage was low and it served me well for 25 years. But after a while, it felt like all I did after I parked my car was walk across pavement and up the stairs into a Habitrail for humans. And though my home didn't have an actual hamster wheel to run on day and night, Metro Atlanta has a way of making you feel like everyone around you is doing just that.

Today, I live in a 100-year old farmhouse in Demorest on eight beautiful acres. Sometimes I have to pinch myself to make sure I'm not dreaming. That's especially true when I see red-tailed hawks circling on updrafts overhead or hear the frogs peeping from the lake. It's then that I feel my heart leap out of my chest and I thank heaven that I live here.

This is what speaks to me now – old barns, big trees, even the small green anole lizard that graces my front porch and is sometimes perched atop the statue of the Virgin Mary as she stands there welcoming me home. I'm not Catholic. I've worshipped in Lutheran churches most of my life, and you don't see statues of the Virgin there. But I love the Holy. I love the Mystery. And my journey has been blessed by that Divine Mystery in ways I'm not nearly as appreciative of as I should be. So when I came to look at this house to rent and saw Mary here, I felt like I was being encouraged by a comforting God to let go of what held me to my old way of living and risk being turned upside down once more.

For fourteen years I visited the northeast Georgia mountains and wished I could live here. But I couldn't make it happen. In 2003, I was downsized from yet another technology marketing job and decided I'd had enough of corporate life. I'd released my first solo CD and was ready to give this music thing a go. So for the last four years I've been on a financial roller coaster (more downs on this ride than ups), surviving by cobbling together musical and speaking engagements with marketing project work. It kind of put a kink in the works when I got nodes on my vocal cords and couldn't sing for eight months last year. That, plus a host of other odd events left me feeling a little battered.

So I finally decided that since I had no security in Marietta, I may as well live where I want to live and have no security. I mean, what's the difference?

My calendar says that December 15 was the first night of Hanukkah – the Jewish festival of lights. That holiday commemorates a time of rededication of the Temple after it had been ruined by enemy soldiers. Even though there was only enough oil to keep the eternal flame lit for one day, it burned for eight days – just enough time to press the olives and consecrate new oil.

So far here, I've found a little bit of work to do but I can't tell yet how long my monetary "oil" is going to last. Yes, it's a little scary to throw oneself at the mercy of the heavens to keep the fires burning, but I love it here. I love that I see familiar faces at contra dancing and at church the next day. I love the sight of moonlight washing over the farm fields. So even though I feel a little looney for unplugging from everything I knew in Marietta, when I see that moonlight, all I can do is pray to be allowed to stay here.

Helping Hands

I'm developing new relationships here in Habersham County (White County too). Most of those relationships have gotten off to a grand start – people have been friendly and welcoming. And, as a newcomer to the community, I really appreciate that. I guess the only relationships I've developed that have been slow to start are those with my new yard maintenance equipment.

When I said goodbye to the condo in Marietta, I also said goodbye to the landscaping service that came with my not insignificant homeowners' association fees. So when the movers unloaded the truck of all my worldly goods, a lawn mower was not amongst them. But in December, that wasn't a top-of-mind concern. In December and January I was just trying to stay warm in this house with the single pane windows without needing to promise a first-born child to the power company. I needed to be frugal, so I kept the thermostat at 68 during the day and used two comforters at night.

But the coming of Spring means the growing of grass, and so I spread the word that I needed a mower. Jerry and Patty, dear friends for the last 25 years and members of my former church, said they'd be happy to give me theirs. It was not being used at the moment, and heck, I could have the weed wacker too.

I've mowed the grass twice now. And though I don't have to mow all eight acres, the area around the house is not small. I know my perspective may change by July, but at least for now, I'm enjoying it. There's a real pleasure in seeing the results of the work.

On the other hand, the tiller and I did not start out as soul mates. Again, I called on my friends – this time Joanne and Bob who live in Sautee. I knew they were long-time gardeners and all 'round handy, whereas this is all new to me. (I mean, I have my gifts, but my handyman skills are still under construction.) They came by and got that tiller humming. And after only a couple of sessions of having my arms nearly pulled out of their sockets, I now have a nice garden spot ready to go.

But see, this is all part of the Grand Experiment of living in the country. Can I put something in the ground and later taste its goodness? I know this is old hat to most people in these parts, but I'm navigating uncharted waters here. And so I was tickled to death when those seeds first sprouted in the tray in my window. Now I'm dreaming of big salads and fresh basil and maybe even a melon or two.

Sometimes I fear if I do something wrong that my little seedlings will dry up and blow away, and my only salads will come from the local grocer. But I know that Life wants to live and that I'm only here as a small-time player in Mother Earth's show. I yearn to be in partnership with her; to become part of the rhythm and flow of this land. It feels like healthy ground to me, like there is good energy here. And I honestly believe that if I show up with positive intention, that life will grow for me in this place.

I had an abundance of wasps in my kitchen not long ago, and at first I'd get the fly swatter. But then I learned that red wasps were not aggressive and so I began to just let them be. We co-existed in peace and I'd let them out when I could. Then today, I rescued a little green anole from the deep waters of my rain barrel. I'd seen him jump in there a few hours earlier and guess he'd had a bit of difficulty getting out (either that or he thought he was at the spa). I always tell him how pretty he is, and when I lifted him out he lingered in my hand for a minute and looked at me. I guess everyone appreciates a helping hand every now and then.

Tell Me a Story

"Tell me a story!" How many times have you heard a child say that? But it's not only children that appreciate a well-told tale. There's something about a good story that makes even us grizzled adults stop whatever we're doing and listen closely.

I didn't realize that the old fairy tales were not really intended for children until I read the book "Women Who Run with the Wolves" by Clarissa Pinkola Estes. In that book, Estes – a psychoanalyst who works in the Jungian tradition – uses a collection of myths and fairy tales to explore deeper psychological truths. That book inspired a whole new direction in my spiritual journey; one that has enriched me in so many ways, showing me the healing power of story.

In the PBS series "Joseph Campbell and the Power of Myth," Campbell said "People say that what we're all seeking is a meaning for life. I don't think that's what we're really seeking. I think that what we're seeking is an experience of being alive, so that our life experiences on the purely physical plane will have resonances within our own innermost being and reality, so that we actually feel the rapture of being alive."

The music I write reflects my own attempts to learn how to feel that rapture of being alive. And so I sing about my journey, about work, love, God, anything and everything that comes. It's all fodder for the mill. I've heard it said that in many Native American languages there is no word for "religion" because the spiritual life was not separate from a person's daily life in any way. So for me, it all gets stirred into the stew.

A woman who'd attended a concert I gave in Covington asked me to sing at her birthday party a few years ago. She'd seen a lot of changes in her life and wanted her party to reflect the sense of awakening she was feeling.

At the start of my second set of songs, because people had been talking at the food table during the break, things felt kind of loosey-goosey. The focused attention I'd had during the first set had become unraveled. I continued to sing and some people were listening and others weren't, and then I came to the part of my program where I wanted to read a story. I'd brought an old Russian fairy tale called "Vasilisa" which is about a girl whose mother dies and leaves her a little doll that will provide her guidance and help when she needs it. It's a metaphor for the development of our intuition, our inner compass system. I wasn't sure it was a good idea to read a story when everyone was so scattered in their attention, but by three minutes into it, you could hear the proverbial pin drop and every person there was transported to another time and place. We were all there together, going for fire to the crone Baba Yaga who lives in the hut built on chicken legs.

The same thing happened at the Mythic Journeys conference in Atlanta last year, where I saw a group of teenagers sitting completely enthralled by storyteller and mythologist Michael Meade. Meade does a lot of work with youth and with elders, using wisdom stories to show us we're not alone in our struggles to find meaning and purpose and rapture.

There is power in a good story, whether that story is true in its facts or only true in its wisdom. I heard that truth again when we read through a rough draft of the community story play being produced at the Sautee Nacoochee Center called "Headwaters: Stories from a Goodly Portion of Beautiful Northeast Georgia." I know the stories that are in these mountains are deep and rich. And I know those stories can heal us. I'm eager to hear more of them.

Steve's Canoe

Taking Care of this Home

The road I live on in northeast Georgia, though busy, certainly offers a lot of beauty. Not really a surprise in a region that has been gifted with what you might call an overabundance of beauty. This is something I celebrate; the landscape in these parts is one of the things that make this place special to me and to many others. But that abundance of grace makes it even more mystifying when I see litter on the side of my road – or any other road.

I guess I just don't understand the mindset of a person who could crumple up their fast food packaging and throw it out the car window and onto the ground, as if that garbage is anyone else's responsibility but their own. As if they don't know those manners are bad. Is the effort it takes to carry that garbage in one's hand or car until you get home really that taxing?

Before I adopted a new five-month-old Lab mix pup from the Habersham County animal shelter, I called my landlord to make sure my having a dog was agreeable to him. We talked about some things to watch out for, and he just asked me to do my best to make sure the dog didn't turn the hardwood floors or window sills into sawdust. I assured him that I would take care of this house as if it were my own.

I guess it's not true that every tenant is as careful as I try to be, and I'm sure there are many landlords who have their share of horror stories about destroyed property or renters who just didn't care. But I love this house, and I love this land and so this place has become a friend. It's a holy place for me, and so I treat it with respect and care.

And call me crazy, but I think this place loves me in return. Every morning I'm treated to choruses of birdsong that are as sweet to me as any church choir. I picked a huge zucchini out of my garden the other day – the first of my harvest – and it sautéed up quite nicely. My taste buds cheered when I sampled the ripe raspberries from the bushes planted by previous tenants. And I express my thanks – out loud – to this house and the creatures around me as much as I can. I want this place to know it is loved.

A few weeks ago, I drove by a church sign that said "Our heavenly home is our real estate." Now I don't feel the need to argue as to whether or not our earthly home is as real as our heavenly home, but if I think about this earthbound life as temporary, then I guess that makes us all tenants, living for a little while in quarters that belong to someone else.

So what kind of caretakers are we of our Creator's earthly property? Do we have a relationship to the ground we walk upon, to the mountains and rivers and even to the grass and trees alongside the road? Or are we uncaring and ill-mannered dwellers who treat the beautiful place we live in as if it's all one big garbage heap?

My guess is that families who have lived here for generations know intimately the land on which they dwell. But I hope the rest of us can find our own way to really falling in love with this place and learn to rest in the embrace of a natural world that longs to love us in return.

Out of the Ashes

There was a fire in a nearby pasture not long ago – seems a tree fell and took a power line with it that then set the grass on fire. Until our recent rains, everything was frighteningly dry and so it didn't take much to get things smoking. Luckily, the fire was out and the power restored pretty quickly and aside from a scorched place in the pasture, everything turned out fine.

I've read that a fire in a forest can spark new growth; the combination of more sunlight getting to younger trees, more air and maybe needed nutrients getting into the ground seems to kick start the life force again.

I think that can happen with people too. We've all known periods in our lives that can only be described as fiery; those times when things get so hot and hurt so badly that we're left as dark as scorched earth. Maybe those fires are sparked by loss, illness, or by changes that we just didn't see coming. No matter the reason, when we're in those furnace times, we usually just want to get out as quickly as possible.

Yet I'm always inspired by people who came out of their own fires with more courage, strength or wisdom then they had going in. Can't we all name people that lived out the definition of "grace under pressure?"

I was amazed several years ago to learn the story of Thomas A. Dorsey (a Georgia native) and his writing of the hymn "Take My Hand, Precious Lord." Dorsey had been a blues pianist, working in bars, until a spiritual healing after a nervous breakdown led him to commit his life to God. The result was the creation of modern gospel music. In 1932 he left behind his pregnant wife to perform at a revival in St. Louis, but after he finished singing he was given a telegram saying she had died in childbirth. He rushed home to learn he had a son. He held that baby all night, but by morning the boy had died. Dorsey was bereft and withdrew from life, until a friend left him in a room holding only a piano. In those quiet moments, the notes to "Precious Lord" – one of the most beloved gospel songs ever – came pouring out.

Recently, I was listening to "A Prairie Home Companion" (as a lifelong Lutheran, it seems a kind of requirement) and Garrison Keillor led the audience in a singing of "It Is Well with My Soul." Horatio Spafford, who penned the lyrics to the song, was also no stranger to fire. He was married with five children but lost his only son in 1871. Just a few months later, the Great Chicago Fire consumed his real estate investments and he lost all his savings. Then, in 1873, the family planned a vacation to Europe. Spafford sent his wife and daughters on ahead so he could tie up some loose ends before joining them a few days later.

The ship on which they sailed collided with another, and 226 people lost their lives. When she reached safety, his wife sent him this heartbreaking telegram: "Saved alone. What shall I do?" He left immediately to bring his wife home, and when his own ship crossed the waters where his daughters drowned, he wrote these words:

When peace, like a river, attendeth my way,
When sorrows like sea billows roll;
Whatever my lot, thou hast taught me to say,
It is well, it is well with my soul.

Out of the ashes; life. Out of the ashes; song. Listen, and you'll hear the sound of faith.

The Roots of Independence

This past Fourth of July, I sadly had to miss some experiences I would have enjoyed. The first was an annual swim party that I've often attended at the home of close friends in Marietta. I would have been able to visit again with people from my former church home and I know the food would have been good, as you can't usually beat church potlucks.

The other thing I missed was being part of the holiday festivities in Demorest. I've never been part of a small-town Independence Day; never sat in a lawn chair on the side of the road while a local parade passed by. And though there might have been a cake walk somewhere in my past, I really would have liked to have seen this one. I have braved horrendous traffic to see fireworks at the Galleria Mall in Cobb County (once and never again) but I thought it would have been a lot of fun to take the cooler to Demorest and spend the day and the evening all in one place.

I really can't complain too much, though, because I got to spend the day celebrating my mother's birthday. My parents flew to Atlanta from Florida and I met up with them at my brother's house where he grilled up a mean batch of ribs. After spending the night at his home, I brought my parents back to Demorest with me for a nice visit.

I have childhood memories of going to the park near my grandmother's house for the fireworks on the Fourth. We would joke that they were all being set off to honor my mother's birthday, but I hated the noise and used to do my best to cover my ears. Back then, I had little appreciation for Independence Day.

I was inspired all over again, though, about the formation of this country while watching as much as I could catch of a series on PBS called "Liberty: the American Revolution." I was most impressed by the seriousness with which the colonial leadership and our citizenry approached the matters being decided. I wonder if we'd be able to draft and debate a constitution like the amazing document created then if we had to do it all over again in this day and age with most people's attention being given to "American Idol," "Dancing with the Stars," and what the Beckhams are doing now that they've landed on U.S. shores.

My mother's mother came over on the boat around 1913 from what was then Czechoslovakia. She was the oldest child in her family and was sent to New York to work as a maid in a household where her aunt and uncle were already working. At only 14 years of age she sailed across the sea by herself and never saw her family or homeland again. She told me she cried for three years. My grandfather was a little older when he came from Poland and he served the United States in both the first and second World Wars (the second time he was no spring chicken, and the Army almost wouldn't take him). My grandparents came to America to find work; to send some meager pittance back to their families. They came to build new lives with only a dream in their pockets. They got married and had six children but lost their second son in World War II.

I just re-read the Declaration of Independence and I'm going to rent that "Liberty" series to watch in its entirety. And I'm hoping I can be in downtown Demorest next year to watch the parade and celebrate Independence Day with my neighbors.

Feed the Soil

A recent project led me to Ed Taylor's farm to talk to him about the local food movement. Ed is an organic grower and he'd been a speaker at a recent workshop at North Georgia Technical College about organic and sustainable agriculture. So when I needed to interview a farmer and hopefully take some pictures of locally grown produce, I asked Ed if I could meet up with him at his Habersham County farm.

The acreage the Taylors own is some of the most beautiful I've seen; rolling hills, creeks and an old cabin and barn. I parked by the barn and hiked down to the bottom land where Ed and a couple of other helpers were harvesting red potatoes. As a new gardener, I have enough trouble keeping up with my tiny vegetable patch, so I was impressed by his many rows of growing things.

I took some photos while Ed continued picking and when he could take a break we walked to a sitting spot and started talking about his farm, about locally grown produce and about the individual and community benefits of buying local food. And I discovered Ed's not just a farmer, he's also a philosopher.

He explained to me that while farmers who use conventional methods focus on the plants – they feed the plants with fertilizer and use pesticides to protect the plants from bugs – organic farmers focus on the soil. "Feed the soil," he said, "feed the soil." He explained to me that if the soil is healthy and vital, the plants will be too. The soil is the ground from which everything springs and if that ground is right and rich with nutrients, what grows from it will be as well.

And isn't that true about life? Ed and I agreed on that, for sure. How can one's life be healthy and good if the ground from which that life springs is poisoned or lacking in the stuff that makes a life thrive?

I realized too late in my garden's life cycle that I'd made a mistake in not testing the soil. I put my seeds and seedlings in a plot where previous residents had gardened and so I assumed it was okay. But then my squash were getting something called "blossom end rot" and my green peppers had brown spots. A bit of Googling led me to the conclusion that my soil was low in calcium. I tried to add lime after the fact, but I don't think it did very much good.

When I packed up my possessions and my cats seven months ago and left Marietta for Demorest, it was mainly because I knew at the deepest part of my being that the soil of Metro-Atlanta was no longer where I could thrive. And I pointed my wagon in the direction of the "evening star" of Northeast Georgia because I'd spent a good bit of time in these parts already. I guess you could say I tested the soil before I transplanted my life.

A friend in south Georgia told me that I could have moved to any small town and would have been okay, that I would have made friends wherever I went. And there's probably some truth to that. I feel I'm a friendly person and I don't think I "put on airs." But I'm not convinced that the pH level of just any old place would have been as perfect for my constitution as where I'm living now. This is good soil, rich soil. And I'm going to do my best to feed it with as much love and care as I can.

Weeding

I hate weeding. It's dirty, sweaty, back-aching work and it's certainly not fun. At least not for me. But the garden doesn't really care if I think it's a good time or not; it still has to be done if I want the good things to grow.

Hindsight being 20-20, if I had to do it all over again, I may not have chosen to start a new garden, begin attending time-consuming rehearsals for a community play and adopt my first puppy all in the same month of May. The wisdom of experience now tells me I may have been biting off a bit more than is reasonably chewable for any one person who's also self-employed and trying hard to make a decent living. But I guess ignorance is bliss, and that combination of chores is exactly what I had in front of me.

So when it came time to make choices, the most vocal and demanding responsibilities of income generation, the dog and the play took first priority. Needless to say, after a while I think I had more weeds than vegetables. I finally had to buckle up and spend a solid two hours pulling weeds.

All of that reminds me of the parable Jesus told about the weeds that grew up among the wheat plants. In the story, the grower sowed good wheat seed, but while everyone was sleeping "an enemy" came and spread weed seeds, resulting in a less than ideal field of grain. The slaves came to the master and offered to pull the weeds, but Jesus said that would result in the wheat being uprooted as well, and so both are left to grow until harvest time.

The pastor of my previous church preached on this parable one Sunday a while back and spoke about how tempting it is to want to "zap" those around us that are like pesky flies in the kitchen. He asked how often we wish that God would just pull out the old bug zapper in the sky and strike down those we feel are bad folks. Or, to stick with the wheat and weed metaphor – wouldn't it be easier if God would just spray some good, strong herbicide on those evil ones?

"Not so fast," said the pastor. And I nodded and cheered silently when he pointed out that the field in the parable is not the world with each of us being either good wheat or bad weeds that need to be separated in some time of judgment. We are each the whole field with both bad weeds and good wheat inside of us. But when is the harvest time for the weeds in our hearts and minds?

There's too much news on the television about people that hurt or kill others because they're angry at the world and their lives are in shambles. Often they've been fired from their jobs, their marriages are failing, and they're quickly sinking in a muck hole of mud and weeds. But instead of looking at their own bad choices and behaviors that caused or contributed to the problems, everyone else around them is blamed. And that approach is tempting for all of us.

I think the time that our inner field reaches its harvest is when we've lived long enough and have become strong enough to withstand the pain and destructive potential of personal weeding. Many times over the last several years I've had to face parts of myself with which I am not pleased. The great psychiatrist Carl G. Jung called those parts our "shadow." Jesus would have just called them our weeds. Either way, the best way to pull them is to start in front of the mirror.

This is My Hometown

I wasn't born in northeast Georgia. I wasn't born in Georgia at all. I was born in a far away northern place where people drink "cawfee" and say "youse guys." A favorite songwriter named John Gorka is from the state of my birth, and he says it this way: "I'm from New Jersey; I don't expect too much; if the world ended today; I would adjust. I'm from New Jersey; no I don't talk that way; I watched too much TV when I was young."

For those whose only knowledge of Jersey is the view from the Turnpike or "The Sopranos" let me say that it's called The Garden State for good reason – if you get off the highway.

It's a very versatile place, in that you can get to mountains, seashore or rolling farmland in a relatively short drive from anywhere in the state. But though I'll defend it as a decent place to be from, I don't ever want to live there again. For all kinds of reasons, some not so easy to put into words, the place where I grew up never really felt like "home" to me. And I've always envied those who had a true family homestead.

I moved to Georgia in 1982 and immediately fell in love with the friendly people I met. It never ceased to tickle me when complete strangers said hello and nodded on the streets of downtown Atlanta. Back then, I used to see a bumper sticker that read "American by birth; Southern by the grace of God." I thought if I could make up my own it would say "Northern by birth; Southern by choice."

A couple of weeks ago, I was invited to sing at a reception in White County to honor the designation of Cleveland, Georgia as a "Better Hometown." And since I pretty much split my time between Habersham and White Counties, I was honored to be asked. But I didn't expect to be inspired. My songwriting well has been kind of dry lately, but that morning I was awakened with a knock from the Muses. And though I mention by name some of the landmarks around Cleveland, the words express how I feel about this whole region. The song is called "This is My Hometown."

A place where people still know their neighbors
And front porch pickin' carries on a breeze
Where fireflies ignite a mountain summer's night
And moonlight paints the pasture and the trees.
In these hills of southern Appalachia

Where Cherokee and Creek ancestors trod
Nacoochee, Mossy Creek to Testnatee and Leaf
Everywhere the handiwork of God.

With mountains rising blue
And rivers rollin' through
A better point of view on holy ground
This is my hometown.

A blend of those who go back generations
And modern pioneers who came today
Something calls us here, something true and dear
It's rooted us in this red Georgia clay.
Now there's no holding back the ways of progress
And change is just a part of every day
But let us keep a hold of all this Nature's gold
So the people down the road can always say

With mountains rising blue
And rivers rollin' through
A better point of view on holy ground
This is my hometown.

The birth certificate that's printed on paper will always say "Elizabeth, NJ" but the one that's imprinted on my heart says "northeast Georgia." For me, "home" is less about where you were born and more about where your soul takes up residence. Welcome home, y'all.

Careful

When Nature Bites

Much of my writing has waxed poetic about the beauty of nature, my love for this place and the land, and of course the wildlife that I see around me. And don't get me wrong, those feelings have not changed. But there's another side to the story, and sometimes it can hurt.

I remember the old television commercials for some kind of margarine where old Mom Nature got a little trigger happy with the lightning bolts when she found out the "butter" wasn't butter – followed by the voice that said "It's not nice to fool Mother Nature."

Now I'll pretty much stop and talk to anything with fur, feathers or even scales (I don't mind snakes as long as I see them first). I've done my best to stay on good terms with the natural world where I live. Last spring, I usually implemented a "catch and release" program with the red wasps rather than swatting them. And I tried to keep a lookout for the little frogs or toads I have around the house whenever I mowed the lawn.

My dog, being a dog, will chase anything that moves. He loves to pounce on bugs and he leaps into the air to get moths. Crickets and grasshoppers are no match for him. But I do not want him killing frogs, so I try my best to keep him away from them. I, on the other hand, can't keep myself from catching them and holding them for a little while. I love to look at them, and I marvel at the ones that are maybe a half inch in length. More often than not, I'm also "baptized" by what they leave behind in my hand.

No matter. I love them anyway.

Yet, I will admit, I draw the line at spiders and several other creepy crawly things. My one-sided "agreement" is that I won't kill them if they stay outside. So I've been known to vacuum up the long legged spiders that set up camp in my kitchen and bathroom.

On the whole, though, I feel I've been quite friendly in my relationship with Mother Nature. So I was kind of surprised when she decided to take a bite.

It happened on an evening when the lawn needed mowing. I've cut my own lawn many times since the grass started growing, but found a guy who'll cut it for me when my schedule got a little crazy this summer. But after the play I was in came to an end, I thought I couldn't justify spending the money and so I got out the lawnmower once again.

There I was, minding my own beeswax, when I must have stumbled through the outer edges of a fire ant mound and suddenly I was doing the Mexican hat dance. Five minutes after they chewed up my ankles, and after I'd hosed off my feet and changed shoes, I was in the same general vicinity of the lawn when I was attacked by yellow jackets. The resulting stings put me in such a state of pain and discomfort that I spent most of that night in the Habersham County Medical Center emergency room. Needless to say, I could have had my lawn mowed about seven times for what I'll pay the hospital.

But the worst was yet to come. Did you know there are caterpillars that cause hives? I didn't know this fact of life until one of those beasts decided to build a home in my bath towel. I will spare you the gory details, but I ended up with a forearm covered in red welts and a fuzzy intruder at the bottom of the tub. So from now on, my "note to self" is to look for teeth and stingers everywhere I go and to maintain a healthy respect for my Mother. And for the frogs, who I fear have cut a protection deal with the fire ants.

Leave the Work Undone

Sometimes the downsides of being self-employed – the unpredictability of my income being the main one – are all that I can focus on. But there are times when I recognize that being the president of my own schedule has its blessings. So when I got a call from my mother telling me that my elderly aunt had had a heart attack and a stroke and was in the ICU, I was glad that I could hit the road without hesitation.

My Aunt Helen is what they used to call a "spinster." And though I cringe at the word, I guess I am too – though I've not yet given up hope that a man I could marry might cross my path one of these days. (a topic for a whole 'nother column, I'm sure) She lived with my grandmother in a house two blocks away from my own childhood home. And though Aunt Helen had quite a fussy streak that was a little scary, I enjoyed our regular Friday night sleepovers. My grandmother would prepare a dinner of pure comfort food and then we'd watch "The Lawrence

Welk Show." Who can forget the angelic voices of the Lennon Sisters, the dance steps of Bobby and Sissy or the accordion magic of Myron Floren?

I have many fond memories of riding in Aunt Helen's Chevy Impala to one of the Jersey beaches – we called it going "down the shore." Seabright or Point Pleasant were two of our favorites. And on occasional summer days, she took me along to her work as an executive assistant at the Airco company. Aunt Helen was a big part of my growing up.

She was rushed to the hospital the day after my parents left for a two-week trip and I didn't want her to be alone in the hospital. Who, I wondered, will take care of me when I'm old if I don't help her out now? It seems like a karma thing to me. If I can be there for Aunt Helen now, maybe someone will be there for me later on.

So I sat in her hospital room, holding her hand and stroking her head when she seemed to be suffering. For a while, I thought she was improving, but her poor heart had taken quite a beating. In some ways, I wonder if her heart hasn't taken a beating for most of her life.

My parents got back home and then we placed my aunt in hospice care. During some of those visits with Aunt Helen in her hospital room, I reminisced about the old days. Even though she wasn't really conscious, I believed Aunt Helen could hear all that I said on some level. And on the night before I left, I told her how important she'd always been to me and said my goodbyes.

But you can't predict with older folks. She's rallied again and has been asking for ginger ale. The nurses call her "feisty" and I can certainly attest to that. Though she's always been a piece of work, she's provided us fodder for so many good stories over the years, that it's hard to keep a count.

I had a soup and sandwich lunch not long ago in a local restaurant. The young man that owns it talked with me about how his business hasn't been quite as good since he'd been gone for some months tending to his dying father. I told him I thought the business would work itself out and that he did the most important thing he could do when he took that time to be with his Dad. I truly believe that some of the work we're most called to do has nothing to do with how we earn our living.

The Dog Park

Not long ago, I took my dog along on a car trip to Florida. I knew I'd be staying at my parents' house, and they're probably Cotton's biggest fans. So we hit the road together and waved goodbye to our mountain home in Habersham County.

My mind was focused on my hospitalized aunt most of the time I was in Bradenton, but I'm always looking for ways to keep my pup entertained, not just for his benefit, but for mine too. I like a dog that's well-behaved, and Cotton is a lot calmer after he's had a chance to blow off some steam with other dogs.

Dogs are pack animals after all. That's one of the reasons I worry so about any dog that's chained outside all day long, or who spends his whole life alone in a pen. Some years back, I volunteered with a pet therapy program in Atlanta, where we took puppies and kittens to nursing homes, and made a fascinating observation at the Humane Society. I was there one Saturday when a new dog arrived. He was a friendly, tail-wagging sort of fellow who came forward to lick my hand. At my next visit, he cowered in the corner, no longer wagging his tail or wanting to be petted. Clearly he had changed drastically over the span of three weeks and I wondered if similar changes occur in people who are put behind bars.

In Bradenton, I asked another pet owner if there was a local dog park and learned that there was – very close to where I was staying. That evening, we made our first visit to the "Happy Tails" park. Little did I know that inside the gate was what surely must be the earthly equivalent of "doggie heaven."

As soon as we entered, several big dogs ran over, surrounded Cotton, and immediately let him know who was boss (and it wasn't him). Cotton's got kind of a teenager attitude – big man on campus – so I think he was a little taken aback to be so put in his place. But I knew it was good for him to learn the ways of the pack.

After two evenings of getting a little heat, I coached Cotton on his need to respect his elders, and to honor the alpha dogs without letting them run him off. After that, all was well, for the most part. But even in the dog park, there were bullies. A couple of canines just had bad attitudes and their owners were pretty lame in their discipline. When those more aggressive dogs were on the offensive, I just took Cotton to a friendlier corner.

Every time we went to the dog park, whether there were five dogs there or 25, Cotton came home happier, more relaxed and I'd had a good time too. It was a joy to watch him tussle and tumble around with a bunch of dogs; to find a friend or two to romp with. And I met some great people – several who were there every night. It became a great social outlet for me as well as for Cotton. I even met a woman with a Bassett hound who later showed up in the ICU as my aunt's nurse. So even though the dog park had its share of bullies – just like any human community – it was easy to see that life is better when you can play with friends.

Staying Afloat

Making a living with music – or with any kind of creative work – has never been easy. I'm at the present end of a very long history of like-minded artists who've had to cobble together a living, adding something to the mix in addition to the art. Musicians and writers have forever served coffee or any number of other part-time jobs to keep themselves afloat.

Maybe if I'd started younger and lived what might have then seemed the romantic life of crashing in my parents' basement while staying on the road all the time to hardly make the gas money it took to go from gig to gig it would have been different. But I came to this leap of vocational faith after having already had health insurance and a mortgage.

Someone who books a concert series told me years ago (before I'd left my last day job) that he only wanted to book musicians who were "full time" at their music and were "100% committed." There are certainly a lot of artists who have gone beyond music as a hobby and I understand the desire to grant the limited number of performance openings to the people who are serious about it. But I wondered later if any of the people that he considered "committed" had spouses or significant others who helped them pay their bills? If they did, then comparing me to them was certainly not an apples-to-apples perspective.

After I'd released my first music CD at the end of 2002, the yearnings for a different sort of life became too strong for me to ignore. I started telling my friends that I wanted to leave my job. But I was waiting for some kind of sign, or maybe a safety net.

In March of 2003, my company bought another company and I learned that several of us were being "downsized" – a corporate way of saying "go home." But rather than being worried, I was thrilled, for I knew this was the sign I'd been waiting for and that it was finally time to get on with my real life.

The years since then have been like that proverbial roller coaster – not a month where I could predict my income. And like my honored "ancestors," I've had to fill in the gaps with non-musical work when needed. But when I got nodes – bumps on my vocal cords – in 2006 and couldn't sing for eight months, it was a real bump in the road. Things got so squirrelly that I decided I may as well move – and so I came to the mountains. But I've wondered for over a year now if Life was telling me that it was time to give up the music and – heaven forbid – get a "real" job again.

I've always thought it a bad idea to fight the current in one's life – that if the energy isn't moving in the direction you want to go, you've got to stay open to a new direction.

Yet walking away from the music felt like the saddest decision I could make. And though the finances have been lean, I have to admit that enough work has always come to keep me going. But I'm once again looking for signs. So it's been heartening to have arts councils around the state suddenly start calling me about bookings.

On a recent trip to Florida, I was swimming in the Gulf of Mexico and was amazed again at how – if I relaxed – the salt water supported me. At one point, I took one of those long, Styrofoam tubes in with me to make the floating a little easier still. And it made me laugh to think that, yes, the ocean of life will support me, but I've got to also do my part. I've got to use my "noodle."

I See Hummingbirds

When Words Fail Us

As I write these words, I am sitting in Bradenton, Florida waiting for Aunt Helen to be moved from the hospital ER to a regular room. Early this morning, the nursing home where she's been living called to say she'd fallen out of bed twice and now was having trouble speaking. All signs pointed to another stroke.

Earlier this week, my dog Cotton and I hit the road south to be with my parents. The Thanksgiving food extravaganza is a holiday that is brimming over with traditions, and it's become my ritual to be here in Florida. After all, no one makes the sausage dressing quite like my mother does – it's a recipe she's modified slightly from my grandmother's, so it's lineage goes way back.

My last trip here in September came unexpectedly when Aunt Helen was hospitalized for a stroke and a heart attack and we weren't sure she was going to make it. But, like a lot of older people do, she rallied and had been improving since I returned to my

Georgia mountain home. She seemed like one of those old boxers who just keep getting up from the mat no matter how hard they've been knocked down.

I proved a bad predictor last time, so I can't know for sure what will happen with her health now. But I'm alarmed at how much trouble my aunt is having in trying to communicate with us. She'll begin a sentence with "I wonder if I..." or "I think I should..." and then the rest of it is gobbledy-gook. My mother and I try our best to make out the words she is saying – "light," "late," "lady" – but mostly it's been impossible. And when we repeat back some of what she said, she looks at us like we're crazy. Like she said the sky was blue and we said her hair was on fire.

Years ago, when I was in college, I saw an incredibly moving play – I think it may have been called "Wings," though I'm not sure. It was about a woman who had been a wing walker during the early years of airplane flight. In her old age, the woman had a stroke and then every time she tried to speak, she thought she was saying one thing but her mouth was actually saying something else entirely. She'd say "I want to wear my sweater" and it would come out "The rosebud is on the ceiling" or something like that. It was heartbreaking to see this woman's struggle, and I could only imagine how frustrating and scary it felt to be inside her body when that body was so uncooperative.

And now I wonder if this little woman who helped raise me is falling down that same rabbit hole to an Alice-in-Wonderland-like world without understandable communication. It's one thing when your brain has shut down to a point where you are no longer even able to imagine sentences; it seems to me it would be even worse to be able to think of exactly what you want to say but to have no means to get those words spoken. That seems to be a sort of mutiny of the mouth.

I have always been a lover of words. I'm an equal opportunity appreciator of silence, but being able to communicate – whether through spoken or written words or through music – is a bedrock part of my personality and my livelihood. And the thought of that ability being stripped away overnight is a terrifying one.

But there is not much I can do for Aunt Helen, except pray. I will do that and tomorrow as we give thanks for the blessings we have received in this year, I will be grateful again for the gifts I have been given and for having the ability to speak and have those words understood. And I will try to remember to say the things that need to be said while I can still say them.

The Founders Would Have Been Proud

One of my preparations for any long drive is to go to the library and look for books on tape or CD to help make the miles go by more quickly. It always works. There's something about being drawn into a story that makes the driving time pass so much more easily. The first time I tried it, I listened to a murder mystery and was almost disappointed to reach my destination before the "whodunit" was solved. I swear I was tempted to drive around the block until I got to the end.

Sometimes I stick with fiction, but just as often, I'll add in an assortment of non-fiction works on topics I'm interested in or from authors I admire. On my last trip to Florida, I was introduced to a novel I thoroughly enjoyed in what is known as the "Elm Creek Quilt Series." This particular story was called "The Sugar Camp Quilt" and happened to be one of the two Elm

Creek novels that is historical in its timing. The novels are set in Pennsylvania, and this one took place during the time of the Underground Railroad, when slaves were trying to make their way north to freedom and some of the Elm Creek residents were offering safe passage.

I guess I was on some kind of freedom theme, without being fully aware of it, since in addition to that Elm Creek audio book, I also picked up one called "American Gospel: God, the Founding Fathers, and the Making of a Nation" and "Whose Freedom?: The Battle over America's Most Important Idea." I've not quite finished the second tape (much more difficult when you're just driving around Habersham County) but both have been excellent and deeply engaging.

Once again, I've been struck by just how unusual this American experiment is in history and in the world. It was radical and progressive thinking in its time to declare that humans were "endowed by their Creator" with the right to be free, to not be beholden to kings or monarchs or feudal lords, and that all people (of course at the time it was only white men) are created equal.

We so easily take for granted what it means to get to that kind of thinking, and seem to forget that we live in a world where a lot of people's allegiance is only to what is good for their tribe or extended family, with no thought about the individual and his or her rights. Our founding fathers (and later, our suffragette mothers and civil rights leaders) somehow developed a mindset that could see this kind of freedom, even though they may not always have been able to live it out completely in their own time (many of our founders kept slaves). In mulling all this over, it strikes me that one can't carry the ideas of freedom without taking seriously things like education, empathy, respect and responsibility – all this is what enables our pursuit of happiness in this land.

A few days ago, I attended my local county commissioners' meeting. They were voting on an ordinance that had created strong feelings on both the "for" and "against" sides of the issue and so the room was packed. Since I had an opinion (not a rarity), I wanted to express it. One of the commissioners commented that he was pleased to see so many people and hoped we would continue to attend their meetings to witness our government at work. I was most pleased that in an age of angrily divisive politics, everyone shared their views with respect and good manners. But the most important thing is that we were there. I think the founders would have been proud.

Winter Blanket

Winter's Own Beauty

I don't like the cold. I would much rather be too warm than too cold. But I guess it's just part of the deal when you live in a house that's a hundred years old that wintertime is going to require a stack of sweaters and thick comforters.

I lived in this house most of last winter (just now coming up on my one-year anniversary here) and, in an effort to save money, kept the thermostat at 68 degrees during the day and 60 at night. Even though the house is very sturdy and well built with new insulation in the attic, the cold air seeps in through the floors and the old-style windows. As a result, two comforters on the bed, thick sweatshirts and a small electric space heater became my new best friends.

Once we hit summertime, I appreciated the tendency of this house to be cool, and I hardly had to use my air conditioner at all until August's heat wave struck. The front porch and the way the sun moved across the sky in its orientation to the house kept me cool most of the day. But here we are again at wintertime, and I can't say I was looking forward to this. Like I said, I'd much rather be too warm.

Of course, the natural world takes a hit at wintertime too. Once the beautiful red and gold leaves have all fallen to the ground, the trees take on a much more barren and stark look and everything gets browner. Cloudy days seem the worst, when a sad layer of grey is painted on top of the brown palette of December.

But – if I pay attention – there is still beauty around me. The red cardinals and the bright bluejays fly from tree to tree or investigate the grass for seeds, adding flashes of color to the landscape. And if I time my morning walks with the dog just right, I may see the Canada geese make a dramatic landing on the lake.

Then, of course, there are those wonderful indoor pleasures that are only available in cold weather. The comforting smell of hot apple cider – the good kind that comes from real apple houses. Or a crackling fire in the hearth when you walk into a place like the Old Sautee Store.

And then there are the holiday decorations and the musical programs that abound. I'm trying to visit as many as I can. Hearing "Breath of Heaven" sung by the angelic voices of the Habersham Central High School Women's Chorus took my own breath away and brought tears to my eyes. And I can't help but smile broadly while driving at night as I come upon an especially raucous house bedecked with festive Christmas lights.

But I think the most beautiful thing I've seen this season comes on the coldest of nights. When the air is so crisp and clear that it goes right through you. On those nights, I groan as I layer up with coat, hat, gloves and scarf in order to take the dog out and brave the falling temperatures. But if I walk far enough into the dark pasture, far enough away from the warm lights of the house, I can turn and look up that hill to the barn. And there, I can see a gorgeous spray of stars hanging like chandeliers above the darker shadow of the barn. Sometimes I can pick out night sky friends like Orion or one of the Dippers. And even though I'm cold, I just have to stay and gaze a while.

New Year, Clean Slate

When I was a kid in my early years at Grace Wilday Elementary School, I was sometimes given the task of cleaning the end-of-the-day dust out of the chalkboard erasers. I'm not even sure if schools still have chalkboards, or if they've all got white boards and dry erase markers now, but I even remember those wire doohickeys that held multiple pieces of chalk so a teacher could draw straight, parallel lines across the board in order to teach cursive writing or musical notes. (Someone told me recently that I didn't look old enough to remember when singer-songwriter Janis Ian was on the radio and I told them I had aged well)

If memory serves me, my job was to take the dusty erasers and beat them against the school's red brick exterior. To this day, I probably have multi-colored specks of chalk dust buried deep in my lungs even though I did my best to not breathe in the clouds I was creating. But I certainly understood that my teachers wanted fresh erasers and a clean slate to start each school day properly.

I feel the same way about a New Year; I'm grateful for the fresh start it brings. See – the end of a year is always a sort of stern scales for me, where I tally up the previous three hundred plus days and see if they lean toward success or not. Of course, everyone's idea of success is different, but my prescription tends to include whether I'm making a living doing work I find fulfilling and whether or not I'm still single. It's that last item that weighs heaviest on the scale.

Being alone is no picnic any time of the year, but it just seems a lot more difficult at the holidays. And so there are times when I want to hold back December like a Dutch boy with his finger in the dike.

Believe me, I do count my blessings – I have family and friends that love me, I have a home to live in that I adore, I have fine furry companions, and I'm still here after more than four years of self-employment. (although if this next year's work doesn't generate a few more green backs, it will not be pretty) Still, December sometimes fills me with dread.

So I always feel a sense of relief when I can tear that old month off the wall and look at the clean slate of January. This simple act means I have 12 new pages of days to work with. I'm hopeful this year that somewhere in these first few sheets of time's passing, I'll finally learn how to have more compassion for myself and not place such stern demands on my human shoulders. Maybe I'll experience a shift of eyesight like the monk Thomas Merton did in Louisville one day when he looked at the people walking around him and saw that they were all "shining like the sun." Or maybe I will be more able to pray his prayer that said, in part: "My Lord God, I have no idea where I am going. I do not see the road ahead of me. I cannot know for certain where it will end...Therefore I will trust you always, though I may seem to be lost and in the shadow of death. I will not fear, for you are ever with me, and you will never leave me to face my perils alone."

For me, being able to pray that prayer in this new year is worth breathing in a little chalk dust as I do my best to clear out last year's disappointments and keep walking forward in faith.

The Empty Seat

Don't Let Your Stories Die

Long before there were books – before the invention of the printing press – people passed their wisdom on through their stories. In fact, in some cultures, that oral tradition was the only way young people could learn about their ancestors, their heritage and about what was important to the folks around them. Those wisdom stories were like a compass; a way of navigating through the dark forests of being human on this planet.

Imagine what life would be like if we had to reinvent the wheel every time a new difficulty arose. If no one had ever recorded and passed on the proper way to deal with illnesses, or injuries, or even fixing a flat tire, we'd either all die young or we'd spend a lot of time on the side of the road.

This passing along of good sense used to be handled not just by one's own parents, but by the other elders of the community. I imagine that helped to ensure that the wisdom you learned was good enough to stand the test of time.

But our culture is all about youth. All about what's "new and improved." We write off everything else as "old fashioned" or irrelevant. We'd rather soak up the messages that come through a flickering television than those that used to come through tales told around a flickering campfire. Maybe that's because we've gotten away from the kinds of rites of passage that the elders of a community used to take their young people through. That loss combined with our natural stage of rebelling against our parents leaves us adrift in a sea that seems to get rougher and rougher with every passing year.

Yet there are mentors out there; we can look for men and women who can provide the bits of fathering and mothering that will help us become wiser. A woman who's been both a mother and a teacher for me is named Chiquita and she lives in Talking Rock. I've known her for more than ten years, and long before I mustered up the courage to pack up my life in Marietta and move to the mountains, I used to recharge my batteries at her beautiful farm.

We'd share food and stories at her dining room table. She'd share the wisdom gained in her journey – the times she was afraid, the times she felt faith and courage, her experiences with love and marriage. All of this fed me in a way that sustains me through hard times even now. And when I call her with successes and I hear how proud she is of what I've accomplished, it's like a tonic that strengthens the very cells of my bones.

We've all got stories that can lift someone else up. The words and images we use to describe what we've seen are like buoys of laughter, tears or inspiration that can literally save somebody's life. But if we keep those stories to ourselves, if we refuse to share them, then we will leave holes in the fabric of our community.

Look – no one likes being preached at. No one wants to listen to an older person who's shaking their finger at you saying "if only you'd done that," or "you should do this." But when someone opens up their heart and says "you know, I felt so alone when I was…" or "when I first laid eyes on my husband to be, it was like fireworks went off all around me" or "here's what it was really like to be fighting a war on foreign soil…" – then I know I want to hear the rest of that story.

Don't let your wisdom die with you. And if you have stories you'd like to bring to the Sautee Nacoochee Center on Tuesday, January 29, they'll be collecting them for upcoming productions of "Headwaters," a story play that I know first hand helps to weave strong threads in this region's tapestry. Call them today and say you'll come. They'll even feed you.

True Nature

My dog Cotton just turned a year old. Well, at least that's as good a guess as any regarding his age. When I picked him out at the shelter last May they thought he was about five months old. So my guess is that our recent snowstorm was his first experience of that cold powder. Now, it's possible that whoever owned him when he was a toddling pup let him play in last February's snow, but I'm doubtful of that.

Cotton's parentage is of course unknown to me. It's easy to tell he's part Labrador Retriever, but when I see the way his fluffy tail curls up, the "eyeliner" around his eyes, and the way his ears kind of stand halfway up before the ends flop over, I've been thinking the other part is either Siberian Husky or German Shepherd. He's an athletic dog with a lot of strength, and there are times I've been tempted to get him a sled to pull to use up some of that extra energy he's generating.

So it was interesting to see his reaction when I let him out after a couple of inches of snow covered the ground the other night. As soon as his paws hit the white, he started racing around like he'd found his true home. I swear it was as if there was some kind of cellular memory deep in his body that recognized the snowy landscape that most Huskies are born into.

All of that got me thinking about the times in my own life when my true nature has revealed itself. When has the discovery of a new place or activity felt like a homecoming to me? Each of us can probably remember more than one of those times, even if we let ourselves get talked out of honoring it. Often it's when we're children – when the walls of "should nots" and "ought nots" haven't been built so tall yet – that we can still see glimpses of the most real parts of ourselves.

For me, one of those moments of recognition came when I first heard the music of Cat Stevens. My mother and I were visiting friends with older daughters at a beach house back in New Jersey and one of the teenagers had brought his then-new album "Tea for the Tillerman." I heard that voice and those songs and everything else around me fell away. While the others all went out to enjoy the surf, I stayed inside, returning the needle over and over again to the first grooves of the record. ("Lisa, Lisa, Sad Lisa, Lisa…")

Later, almost every evening, I would walk my childhood dog to the nearby golf course. We'd pass the suburban houses crowded together, cross the creek, squeeze through a hole in the fence and find ourselves walking on the greenest carpet of grass I'd ever seen. I'd take my shoes off just to feel the velvety softness and we'd run around, ducking under groves of pine trees whenever the maintenance guys would go by. I remember one time looking up into the eyes of a barn owl and again feeling that sense of time standing still.

So it's no wonder that I find myself happiest now when I'm mixed up in something musical or enjoying wildlife in the natural world. And though it may have surprised my friends and family when I ran away from Atlanta to live in the mountains, it was no surprise to me because I felt just like Cotton in the snow the first time I saw the Sautee Nacoochee Valleys in 1991. And I knew I had to do whatever it took to be here in this place, because though I may have been birthed in suburban New Jersey, I'm a breed of girl whose true nature is only really home here in northeast Georgia.

Habersham Mills Lake

Frozen Lake

We recently averted disaster here in Habersham County. One cold morning not long ago, after a string of early temperatures in the teens, I discovered the lake that I live near was almost completely frozen over. Having a lake that's turned to ice was not the disaster. It was the near miss of losing our lake to White County that I was worried about.

I know it was a close call because I heard the cracking sound when the ducks who were on the lake took off as they heard my approaching footsteps. I saw the only spot not frozen and the ripples that indicated recent movement and so I knew that's where they'd been. And I've heard that old tale about a lake that froze so fast while the ducks were swimming in it that when they flew up into the air, the lake went with them and was later dropped on some faraway place. I can't attest to the truth of that old yarn, but I'm just glad we're not down a whole lake on this side of the Chattahoochee River.

Seeing frozen bodies of water is not common here in Georgia, though I've seen them often enough in other parts of the country. I grew up in a place that saw regular snow and ice in the winter and I remember many days walking to school when I would step gingerly to avoid a serious wipeout.

While other kids took running starts to get maximum "slideage" on the slick sidewalks, I was never one to fling my body through space at high speeds – at least not on purpose. It wasn't like I ever broke a limb or a tooth; it was just that I hated the idea of losing control of my feet. Feet, after all, are what keep us grounded. And I was always a kid who wanted to know where I stood.

So it was a big deal for me to work up the nerve to take ice skating lessons at the rink in my town. And though I was never able to complete graceful figure eights, I did manage to learn enough to stay vertical more often than not.

Until, that is, I decided to put in some extra practice time on a nearby frozen lake. For some reason that evening, no matter how I approached my turns, I ended up losing my footing and hitting the ice. With my hip. My left hip. Every time. Needless to say, after a few of these rounds of "lake vs. human" kept finding me on the losing side, I'd had enough.

But there was another experience of ice that I treasured in those years. That was when I would head out to our backyard after a winter storm and plow through the mounds of snow to peel the ice from our rhododendron plants. If I was careful, I could collect perfect reproductions of leaves that looked more like glass and then hide them in a tiny "igloo" I would fashion out of snow bricks. It always amazed me to see the delicate patterns of lines in the ice that would be left by the leaf veins.

That same kind of beauty fascinated my niece when she visited me the day this lake froze over. Like me when I was her age, she never tired of finding thin plates of ice glass covering the ground, and examining them for pretty patterns. At the lake, the sound the stones made thrilled us as we skipped them across, chirping out like birds. And since I knew we'd only hear this sound again the next time rock could meet frozen lake, I was glad that water kept its footing even when the ducks flew away.

Mercy

A good portion of my childhood days were spent trying to rescue wounded creatures. I can't say that all my efforts were helpful, but I was always moved to at least try. So for many years, I carried home an endless parade of wounded birds and homeless kittens. Even picking up a nasty case of ringworm from one of the small cats didn't put a dent in my activities.

Of course, some of the wild birds didn't make it out alive and I can't say for sure if that was due more to their poor health or my poor knowledge of bird care. There was even one for which I donned the hat of "flight instructor" and I can still see myself in the backyard, tossing the bird up into the air and watching it flap its wings while it coasted to the grass. After one spectacular launch, it landed in the shrubbery and vanished. A long search turned up no clues as to the fate of the mysterious disappearing bird.

It's hard to know for sure what created this need to rescue those with fur or feathers. From the start, I was nutty about animals and much preferred the stuffed kind to dolls for my playthings. After high school, I even set out to be a veterinarian but a cranky experience with college chemistry derailed that engine.

Maybe the need was as much a response to the powerlessness I'd felt when it came to rescuing my emotionally wounded father. I know I'm not the first person whose later life path was guided by seeds planted in a troubled family environment. So on a recent day when I heard the pain-filled yelping of a dog, I just had to try to help the creature that I knew must have been hit by a car. I drove up my road and down again, but, just like with that long-ago bird, I found no dog, injured or otherwise.

In one of the old stories, a lawyer who wanted to test Jesus asked him what he must do to inherit eternal life. The lawyer proudly recited from Scripture all about how one must love God and love your neighbor as yourself. But then he asked, "And who is my neighbor?" As if there were some humans that deserved help and some that did not. As if Jesus would teach that we should only care for those that are in our family, or who live next door; those whom we already like – and no others.

As usual, Jesus answered with a parable; a symbolic story meant to teach a larger truth. He told about the man who'd been beaten and left in the road for dead. At first, the kinds of people that the lawyer would have respected walked right by, turning their heads and their hearts away. But then a Samaritan – an ethnic group long held in low regard as enemies of the group to which the lawyer belonged – paused in his journey, refused to look away, and carried the wounded man to help. Which of these three acted in a neighborly way? The one who showed mercy.

A day or two after hearing the painful yelping, I was driving again, and came around the curve to suddenly notice a large white dog lying in the grass about ten feet off the road. My heart broke as I realized this must be the animal that I'd heard. I drove home in tears of sadness, anger and frustration. Who hit this dog and then just left him here? Why didn't I find him the day I looked? Why was I not given the chance to save this animal's life, or at least to keep it company as it passed from this world?

Though my questions – both past and present – may never be answered, I know one thing for certain. That dog was my neighbor.

Waiting for You

Back Roads, Small Towns

Not long ago, I had the opportunity to pack my suitcase and guitar in my Honda CRV, drive south on Interstate 85 and then Interstate 185, and exit onto Georgia Highway 520 to head to the tiny town of Dawson for a performance in a beautiful place called the Main Street Theatre.

When the organizers of this show contacted me about doing a concert for the senior citizens in their community, I had never heard of their town and would have been hard pressed to locate it on a map. But their email was most welcome, as it came at a time when I wondered if the well of gigs for this singer-songwriter had dried up as much as Lake Lanier last fall.

In fact, just a few days after I'd posted this Dawson concert on my website, I heard from the arts council in Ft. Gaines saying they were only an hour away from Dawson and would I want to perform in their community on the same trip? These days it's getting harder and harder to afford to take long car drives, but these were the kind of gigs musicians love to get – where the sponsors actually cover things like mileage and the cost of hotel rooms. So I left my mountain home for a 250 mile trip to southwest Georgia with little idea of what I would experience in those places.

I do have an appreciation for interstates and the speed of travel that they allow, but if given the chance and the choice, I much prefer to drive a winding back road that passes through small towns and farm fields. As I got closer to my destination, I realized that I'd have to make plans to return soon so I could visit destinations like Westville and Providence Canyon – places that have been on my "must see" list for a long time.

I'm generally a safe driver, but I have to admit that I was doing a lot of neck craning every time I passed an old house, or a grove of pecan trees or even a field of cotton plants that still had a few wisps of white clinging for dear life. That's what feels real to me; not asphalt exits that all look the same.

I was a little early and a lot hungry arriving in Dawson, so I called Rhonda at the theatre and asked where she'd recommend I have lunch. I'll visit a fast food chain restaurant if that's all there is, but I'd much rather try some "home cooked" local fare. Rhonda said the place to go was Mrs. Paul's restaurant and so there I was with a plate of catfish, cornbread, sides and sweet tea. I assumed everyone in the place probably knew each other, and none of them knew me, so I smiled and said hello to the people around me and we struck up some conversation.

A few of those folks even came to my show later that afternoon, though Rhonda told me a genteel woman told her that she thought it was just "vulguh" to call this a "senior citizens show." Maybe she hated the idea of admitting she was of a certain age to attend? But all were welcome and they came and loved every song I sang – from the original ones they'd never heard to "Sentimental Journey" and "Moon River." Many even sang along. And after reading some of my writing where I talked about my dog Cotton, a woman told me later that she wished she could meet him.

Afterward, I drove west to perform the next night at George Bagby State Park in Ft. Gaines and had a similar experience with welcoming people and a great show. And there, a small group of us even had our own "after concert" gathering in the graceful home that Ken and Ann had restored with such care and attention to beauty, surrounded by trees draped in Spanish Moss.

I've been laughingly referring to this trip as my "Tiny Towns Tour." Most days, I keep my eyes open for opportunities to share my music and my stories in lots of different places, from clubs to churches to festivals, but I'd take more shows in small towns on Georgia back roads in a heartbeat. As long as the sweet tea keeps flowing.

Red Birds of Grace

Every time I look out my back window to where the bird feeder stands and see the cardinals, it gets me thinking about grace. Not grace as the kind of short prayer we say before we eat a good meal, but grace as a surprise gift from the heavens.

Growing up in the Lutheran church, we used that word grace quite a bit, and I think I know what it means but I wondered how I might explain it to someone who'd never heard it before. So I popped online and searched on the word in Wikipedia. The listing said that the word in the Christian New Testament that is usually translated as "grace" is the Greek word "charis" which literally means "that which affords joy, pleasure, delight, sweetness, charm, loveliness."

I would without hesitation apply those terms to the cardinals that live at my house. For me, winter would be a lot harder to survive if it weren't for the moments of joy I experience when I see those flashes of bright red. Their color is so brilliant, so rich, that just seeing one in a tree bare of leaves can make a dreary day a little brighter.

So you can imagine my joy when I look at the bush next to the magnolia tree and see not one, not two, but eight or ten cardinals all perched there! That just seems like an abundance of grace that is way over the top.

I experienced a similar feeling when I spent a few days earlier this year in silence at the Monastery of the Holy Spirit in Conyers, Georgia. It had been a very hard and sad December for me – for a lot of reasons – and once we rang in the New Year I just felt the need to leave behind all the distractions of telephone and email for at least a few days.

The Monastery was established in the 1940's when a group of Trappist monks traveled to Georgia from Kentucky to build a new community. It's a beautiful place with a lake, ducks and geese, and the beauty continues inside as well, especially in the cathedral with its soaring ceiling and stained glass windows.

Retreatants that come to the monastery are welcome to join in any or all of the worship services led by the brothers, but what felt most holy to me was the last service of the evening that began with the monks' chanting in a deep darkness broken only by candlelight.

When your soul is carrying heavy burdens, the evocative beauty of holy ritual can lift those burdens like steam rising from a comforting pot of tea. Holy moments of synchronicity kept tapping me on the shoulder, showing me over and over again that God saw me and knew my heart. And after a Divine accident put a book in my path that brought tremendous healing, I knew once again that I had been touched by Grace.

We humans like to think that we can control our lives. We like to think that we can earn our way to heaven or that if we are "good enough" we will be granted a good life free from pain or chaos. But we will never understand this life; we will never understand the mystery of it all. And we will never be able to predict or control the flow of it – we can't push the river.

By the time I got to the monastery all I knew was that something in my interior life had to shift in order to set me free from the chains of perfectionism and the need to control everything. The online encyclopedia says that "the grace of God is something that upsets settled human notions about merit, about what is deserved, and what is due as recompense." I don't know what I thought I deserved, but what I experienced in the silence of that sanctuary in the flow of love that washed over me was pure Grace, pure Gift.

The Perfect Egg

There's just nothing better for breakfast than a good fried egg – over easy is my preference – with toast for dipping up all that creamy gold nectar of the gods. And I know my waistline may not agree, but I think eggs fried in anything but real butter are just heresy. If it's a scrambled kind of day, then the butter flavored spray will do, but if I'm going to hope for unbroken yolks then I feel the real thing is an absolute must.

For most of my life, I was content with buying my eggs from the local grocer, taking the time to open the carton and shift each egg individually in its resting place to make sure they weren't cracked. My mother always taught me that if an egg held fast in its cradle, then it was likely broken and leaking out a bit at the bottom. And while growing up in busy suburbia, I would never have considered eating brown eggs, thinking their color must surely make them taste weird or at least different from what I wanted to be tasting.

But all of that changed when I started buying eggs freshly laid by neighborly chickens. To be honest, the event that began my whole conversion to preferring local fresh eggs happened while I was visiting my friend Chiquita on her farm in Talking Rock.

Chiquita has been a frequent adopter of water fowl that have been left at nearby animal shelters, and so she's always got a collection of ducks and geese camping out at her place. One morning we were walking around the lake and came upon a nice little duck egg just lying there in the grass as pretty as you please. Chiquita knew it was fresh, so she encouraged me to pick it up and take it inside for breakfast. I was a little bit shocked at the prospect, as I'd not been in the habit of cooking things I found lying on the ground, but in we went, toting our small treasure.

When I cracked that egg in the pan, I was surprised at the deep orange of the yolk. And when I tasted it, I knew I'd discovered something very important that I'd been missing out on for a long time.

It's possible that I could have located a source for local eggs when I lived in Marietta, but I'd not come across any. So when I moved to the mountains, I was eager and ready to visit a nearby farmer who could sell me some of those perfect eggs. I even started getting the state farm publication to be better informed. But first, I was very curious as to why some eggs are white and some are brown.

I learned online that different breeds of chicken lay different color eggs, and that you could tell what color eggs a chicken will lay by the color of its ear lobes. Ear lobes? Chickens have ear lobes? This was news to me. I'm learning a lot living in the country. I've also learned that eggs laid by chickens who get to roam around, eating bugs and grass and such – what's typically called "free range" – have less cholesterol and more of the good stuff than mass-produced eggs.

Last year, I'd found a family not too far away that had chickens and I'd been buying some of their extra eggs, but then their chickens died. Just recently I found a carton of eggs at the grocery that were from North Carolina and they were excellent, but not in stock at my last visit. Here I am in search of the perfect egg yet again. So if any yard chickens in Habersham County have eggs to spare, I'd certainly love to hear about it!

Two

A True Friend is a Treasure

On the morning following what was probably the best spring-like day we'd had yet this year here in northeast Georgia I boarded a plane at the Atlanta airport headed for Chicago. I held no illusions that I would find spring-like weather there. What I knew I would find was a treasure that means more to me than a good spring day – a true and loving friend.

I first met Laurel a few days before my first semester of college classes began at Purdue University. As an out-of-state student, I'd already moved my things into one of the dorm rooms in the suite I'd been assigned to; but as we got closer to class time, other freshman girls were moving in as well. Laurel arrived with her parents and older siblings who were already attending Purdue, along with her brother's roommate to help lug the heavier items. Up to this point, it had seemed like the belongings of other girls materialized out of nowhere – unattached to their owners who'd drop off a load and then go back to their homes in Indiana towns not too far away. So Laurel was one of the first of my suite mates that I'd actually met.

Being a bit shy in this new environment, I didn't say much as she chose an as-yet-unoccupied room but after we talked non-stop for an hour I eagerly exclaimed that she just had to move in with me. I could tell immediately that Laurel and I were going to be great friends.

Author John O'Donohue, who wrote about Celtic Spirituality until his premature passing not long ago, used the term "anam cara" which in Gaelic means "soul friend." I can't claim Celtic heritage on any day other than St. Patrick 's Day (when we're all Irish at heart), but I understand what a soul friend is and I know that they are rare.

It had been about five years since I'd seen Laurel and during this visit, like all our others, it was as if time melted away and there had been no gaps at all in our time together. On the other hand, it's not easy to embrace the way time marches on and we had a hard time accepting the grey hairs coming in or the fact that she now has sons that are older than we were when we met.

Here's what my experience tells me is true about soul friends – we laugh a lot in their presence; we can tell them anything; we love who they are, flaws and gifts together; and time spent in each other's presence flies by way too fast.

I was heartbroken when I had to go, and not because the weather there was finally becoming bearable, but because it's hard to leave behind someone with whom you feel you can be more yourself than you can with most anyone else. I spend way too much of my time focused on serious things and wrestling with harsh internal voices that demand perfection from myself and the world around me. I don't give myself nearly enough permission to just be open-armed and open-hearted to the life flowing toward me. But when I'm with this soul friend, there's a lighter energy streaming in that illuminates all those sadder places in my heart and fills me with joy. I find parts of me coming out to play that I hadn't seen in a long time, and that is a state of being that I want to hold on to.

I know I should be grateful that I have a kind of friendship in my life that many people might never experience at all, but it's hard to not want more of that light. Life is just so much better with good companions to join us on the journey.

So now we're looking for ways to get together on a more regular basis. I'm thinking an annual girls' weekend in Kentucky might be just the ticket.

Working with Beauty

I had the pleasure not long ago of presenting a program of music and stories called "Working with Beauty" to a large group of businesswomen in White County for a Chamber of Commerce event. The title of my program came from a song I wrote several years ago of the same name that is a musical exploration of the idea that "making a life" rather than just "making a living" can only happen when we bring our whole selves to our work. That just maybe – if we could find a way to bring mind, hands, heart and soul into our jobs – work could actually become a juicy thing of beauty rather than just some dry and tasteless routine.

One place I know that is overflowing with examples of beautiful work is the John and Mabel Ringling Estate in Sarasota, Florida. My parents live near the site, and we've gone there several times on my many visits to Bradenton. The first time I entered the art museum years ago, I was immediately captured by the huge Rubens paintings in one of the great halls. Rubens is one of those masters who was able to paint in such a way that light seems to stream right out of the colors. He painted on a truly grand scale.

But it was something on a much smaller scale that really wowed me on my last trip to the Ringling Estate. In the learning center there are the stunning fruits of a lifetime of working with beauty by a man named Howard Tibbals. Tibbals fell in love with the circus at an early age and began creating miniature models of circus life after he was given woodworking tools by his parents.

Fifty years later, he completed a replica of the Ringling Bros. and Barnum & Bailey Circus, circa 1919-1938, complete with "eight main tents, 152 wagons, 1,300 circus performers and workers, more than 800 animals and a 59-car train." Even in its ¾-inch-to-the-foot scale, it still takes up 3,800 square feet of space.

My jaw kept dropping as I walked from scene to scene in the lovely diorama that housed Tibbals' creations. Each performer, each animal, each prop and wagon was perfect in every detail. As I glanced around, I could see that everyone there – young and old alike – was as entranced by this gorgeous display as I was.

I knew without a doubt that the man behind this tiny circus was absolutely in love with his work. I don't know how Tibbals made his living, but it's clear that the years this man spent bent over his work tables, ignoring sore muscles and eye strain, were filled with passion and purpose.

These are the lyrics to the chorus of my song "Working with Beauty" —

Is this any way to make a life or just a living?
Can we really reach the top by serving just the bottom line?
If we could bring our hearts and souls to the work we do,
  Wouldn't we be working with beauty?

While in college, I read a book by Studs Terkel called "Working," which contains interviews with people from all kinds of jobs talking about their work. It has stuck with me all these years later that one of those women he interviewed said that she felt that most people's jobs were "too small for their spirits."

That's exactly how I felt for many years working in various software marketing jobs. They kept my bills paid and my brain engaged, but I think my heart and soul mostly stayed home when I put on that suit of corporate clothes each day and battled metro Atlanta traffic to some high rise office building.

Today, my work as a performing songwriter and speaker certainly carries its own share of challenges, but it can also carry my passion, my joy, and my hopes that the people I encounter will be touched or inspired in some way to live more deeply into their own lives, and then bring that depth of spirit to the people they touch in their own work – paid or unpaid.

Asking for Help

We live in a culture that celebrates self-sufficiency. And that's not usually a bad thing. After all, our parents would not really be doing their jobs if they launched us into the big world without the tools we need to take care of ourselves.

Many years ago, I was at the home of friends when the mother of the household instructed the girls to make the boys' beds. I wondered why the boys couldn't make their own beds, as the young adults involved were all about the same age.

For a brief time after my older brother moved to Georgia, he lived with me in my Marietta condo. We had opposite work schedules – which was probably a blessing in disguise – but now and then we were home at the same time where I occasionally witnessed him cooking, doing laundry or ironing his own shirts. I was proud that he was able to master all those chores that are often termed "women's work," and knew that being self-sufficient in these things would serve him well throughout his life. After all, it has seemed like pure folly to me for anyone to assume that there will always be someone else around to take care of life's basic necessities.

On the other hand, I know that women who have been married a long time and raised children often find it nearly impossible to let anyone else take care of them. I was once on a spiritual retreat where volunteers who took serving roles were happy to wait on us "pilgrims," seeking to meet our every need; and, in the process, nearly creating panic attacks in some of the women present.

In a similar-but-different way, I've found that when you've been single most of your adult life, it's easy to take self-sufficiency to the extreme. And when you take pride in being a capable, industrious adult it can almost be painful to ask for help. Isn't it surely a sign of weakness when we can't completely take care of ourselves and our own needs?

I've never wanted to "owe" anyone anything, and so for most of my life, I've tried my best to just "soldier through" any obstacles I've encountered and go the distance on my own. But I've come to believe that it robs us of community when we don't reach out to those that care about us to let them come to our aid. It's part of our nature to want to help, and being able to help another builds a kind of personal connection that wouldn't be made otherwise.

So when I had 200 envelopes that needed to be stuffed with music CDs and promotional materials and mailed to radio stations around the country, I decided to call in some of those many hands that are known to make light work.

I put the word out to several women friends and told them if they came to help I'd provide the pizza. One friend couldn't make it at the designated time, but she came on her own a little early to help me with the preparatory work. Then later that evening, a small group descended with ready hands and smiles on their faces. We made a party of it. And in a kind of "multiplication mathematics of love" we experienced a shrinking work time and a great growth in fellowship and laughter.

Just before everyone walked out the door, one of the women offered to lead a blessing over the boxes overflowing with fat envelopes so that a good spirit and positive energy would travel with my offerings as they made their way through the U.S. Postal Service. So we circled around, joined hands, bowed our heads and prayed. I was moved, awed and humbled by this gesture of grace and generosity. And I imagined small wings like those of angels carrying my music out into the world, where I hoped my songs would touch the hearts and lives of people who might be hungry for just a bit of inspiration.

Hidden Gems

I just returned to my office from the nicest little mid-week picnic I've had in a long time. My refrigerator held a bit of leftover homemade meatloaf and red-skin-potato-salad, and so I called a friend who works in Cornelia this morning to ask if I could swing by with a picnic. Did he know of any outdoor tables somewhere nearby? He said he did, so into the cooler went the meal, some Cokes and a couple of brownies.

First, we drove to where the "big red apple" sits near the train depot and there were some fine cement tables there, but then my friend said he wanted to check out a different place that might be worth a picnic. We drove through town where all the street-scaping work is being done and came to a little spot with a lot of trees called the Irvin Street Park. If you blinked your eyes, you'd drive right past it. We had to crane our necks to verify that there were, in fact, tables where we could eat there.

Once we left the car and the asphalt behind and headed down the wooden stairs, we came upon a sweet little spot that was just beautiful. Shaded tables sat along a tiny creek, a swing hung beneath the limbs of a great tree and there was even a swishing waterfall just a little ways down that we could hear making its sweet music. I wondered how many people in Cornelia are even aware that this lovely gem is hidden right beneath their noses?

These days, I work in a home office with a view of my old barn that's pretty hard to beat. At any time, I can step outside to shake the cobwebs from my brain and clear the eye strain from too many hours at the computer. And I never stop appreciating that.

But I know there are lots of folks who work in windowless offices or cubicles – or worse – day in and day out with only the same tired view of toothpaste colored walls. For most adults, the days of afternoon recess are over. Who has the time anymore to sit and listen to bird song or the breeze in the leaves when there's always so much work to be done?

That's the thing, though. There will always be more work to do. It will never all be done. The flow of paper will never quit. The demands on our hours, our brains, our lives will never let up – that is, unless we say "enough is enough." Even if for just one brief hour.

My last full time job in Atlanta was located near Perimeter Mall and it's hard to find a place that is more driven than that spot. Between the office buildings and the shopping and all the never ending traffic, it's easy to get sucked into the vortex that says that speed is the only thing that matters. Or the trap that says every person should be reachable by email, phone, laptop or Blackberry at every given moment of any given day.

That is a lie.

We have lives to live that do not turn on the flow of commerce. The cells in our bodies and the moments in our days do not belong to the boss. Sure, we make an agreement to give the work our time in exchange for the wages we are paid. But our peace of mind and interior wellness cannot be bought and sold.

So, wherever you work, whether in Cornelia, Atlanta or elsewhere, let me encourage you to do a little exploring. Find yourself just one little patch of green space. One small grove of trees that you can sit under, even if you bring your own lawn chair. And whenever you can, take your lunch out into the shade and breathe a little slower. Savor every bite you take. Feel the grass under your toes. Listen to the world around you. When you get back to the job, you and your work will be the better for it.

Down, Not Done

I don't know what did it. I don't know what pulled the tree at the edge of the pasture up by its roots and laid it on its side. Probably a great gust of wind blew by, like they tend to do in this place, and that was enough to take the tree down. Whatever it was, it happened before I lived here.

I'd noticed the laying down tree before the other day. I've often walked by its roots sticking up into the air every which way like a bad hair morning. And I guess I just assumed it was dead. Out for the count. A casualty of who knows what storm.

So I must have done a double take last week when I looked up the hill and saw for the first time that this laying down tree was completely leafed out with a full "head" of green "hair." I guess just like Mark Twain, that tree's comments from the ground might be all about how the "rumors of my demise have been greatly exaggerated."

If we have eyes to see, Mother Nature gives us an endless stream of good lessons, and I guess I would learn from this tree that just because something or someone is down, it doesn't mean they are done. That even when a life has been pulled up by its roots and thrown to the ground, it doesn't mean that life no longer has purpose or beauty to it – as long as there's still a connection to the deeper source of Life.

Though the trunk of that tree hit the ground pretty hard, it's obviously still got some roots digging down below the surface appearance of things that are bringing it the nutrients it needs. And it still continues to reach out above ground too – toward the sun's light. Because of all that reaching down and up, I'm sure the tree is still providing homes for birds and other critters that need shelter, plus any number of blessings for the bugs. The flow of life that circles around from one to the other is still at work, even when it doesn't seem likely or possible.

I think it's like that with people too. Even when others might think we're past our prime or that we've been taken out of the game through injury or illness or age, we can still participate in the great flow of Life and Love that is happening around us every day.

A great example of that is my new friend Verna. Verna is 101 years old and lives in one of the Magnolia Hills assisted living apartments. I heard that she enjoyed my writing and wanted to meet me, and so I went to see her. And from the moment we met, she has been one of the greatest advocates and supporters of my writing that I have ever had.

Verna is a great tree that has seen a lot of life, and though she gets around surprisingly well for her age, she's probably not standing quite as tall as she used to when she was a young woman living in uptown Atlanta. She's begun to tell me some of the stories of her life, and I get the impression that she was quite the mover and shaker in her day.

Today, Verna moves with the help of a walker. But it doesn't matter. She holds my hand and pours her love into me and I am lifted up by just knowing her. Every time I read her an especially good turn of phrase, she tells me how much she enjoys hearing something said in a new way. I love that she is still curious and interested in learning.

Verna may, in some ways, be lying down like my tree but she is not done with the reaching out part of her life. And that, my friends, is true beauty.

The Garden of Relationships

This time of year, as I drive around the county, I can't help but notice my neighbors' vegetable gardens. It's true that I have a bit of "garden envy," since all I planted this year was a couple of tomato plants. I just didn't have it in me to go all out with a full garden. Instead, I can't help but admire the ever-taller corn and ever-wider squash bushes that I see through my car windows. And let's not even discuss the sugar snap peas that I'm sure others have been enjoying. It's almost too much for me to bear.

So you can't blame me when I start applying garden metaphors to everything. It's just that between the sowing, the weeding, the tending and, eventually, the harvesting, the lessons we learn in the garden seem to be useful in so many areas of life. And I say that as a true novice to the gardening world. I'm sure the experts out there could list countless more similarities than I can.

The latest comparison that's grown from the "soil" of my mind is that dating and love relationships are like gardens. Now the ground of relationship metaphors has been plowed many times over – after all, who can hear the terms "Mars" and "Venus" anymore without thinking about men and women? But rather than travel to outer space for relationship guidance, I'm happier to dig down into the dirt of it all. So here's my take on things.

I think when two people find themselves in a dating relationship and have an interest in getting closer, that it's as if they have decided to plant some good seedlings together in the hope and with the optimism that they can eventually harvest something tasty to eat together.

Of course we know that not all gardens flourish. In some cases, the soil just didn't have the right nutrients to begin with, or hail storms come unexpectedly to wither a summer's work. But for sure, if we want to increase our chances of a healthy garden and a good harvest, there are some basic practices we'd be wise to follow.

In the world of real tomatoes and beans, it's possible for one gardener to grow a healthy garden, if it's not too big for that gardener's back and hands to keep up with. But from my perspective, a relationship garden can't grow with only one gardener. If all the tending is left in the hands of one set of garden gloves, it's not a relationship – it's just a salad bar.

I've known more than a few people who kept trying to draw their spouse's attention to the bugs eating the zucchini, or to a need for more or less water, or more or less fertilizer over the course of many years in their marriage gardens. But no matter how often they asked their partners to give the garden the attention it needed, their pleas fell on deaf ears (and I'm not talking corn here). Yet those same absent gardeners expressed shock and outrage when their spouses finally gave up and left to search for greener pastures. Love cannot thrive if one is not willing to bend even a little to the needs of the garden.

No, the love only blossoms when two pairs of hands do the tending together; when two pairs of eyes notice the tenderness of the new leaves and the beauty of the squash blossoms; when two noses smell the dirt just after a good rain. It's the presence – the full presence – of the twosome that creates the alchemy that makes the magic happen, that makes the symphony in the biting of the crunchy pea pod or the sweetness of that homegrown tomato explode in the mouth like a Fourth of July fireworks display. With relationships, as with gardens, if we want to reap the rewards we must put our hands in the soil.

Rivers of Stories

As witnessed about this same time last year, rivers of stories are flowing again out at the Sautee Nacoochee Center. My participation in the premiere production of "Headwaters: Stories from a Goodly Portion of Beautiful Northeast Georgia" was, for me, one of the highlights of 2007, and so I didn't hesitate when it came time to sign up again. And just like last year, something like forty of us have signed over a goodly portion of our time and energy for the months of June and July in order to bring this community story play to life.

And live it does. This play isn't some collection of dusty history-book chapters that might make one sleepy eyed. No, the stories that have been collected from counties in this region – some historical, but mostly contemporary – are fully alive and kicking. Rather than snores, these stories evoke smiles, laughter and sometimes even tears. Yes, the waters are flowing again.

One of the stories in "Headwaters" that has always touched me the most is about a family with a handicapped child and the way the community poured out their love and labor in order to build a ramp, a bed and install a hot tub so that life for this family could be a bit easier. I play one of the characters in those scenes – a woman who helped to rally the neighbors to come together in this way.

The woman my character is based on was again part of the rallying team that surrounded a gifted and much beloved man in the community after he learned this spring that he was dying of cancer. I did not know Marlin well, but through Julianne's writings, I became a witness to his breathtakingly beautiful and amazing journey to his heavenly home.

Despite what we see on the evening "news at 11," and though flawed we may be, we humans have great love and altruism within us. And this is how we know we are human and how we know what is inside of us – we tell our stories.

"Headwaters" has so many wonderful stories; stories about rivers, fishing, bears, and also about the dismantling of segregated education and about what being marked as a "woods colt" (an illegitimate child) meant in the early 1900's in these parts.

In coming to know the stories of a place, one comes to know the place itself and its people. I've heard so many folks both in the cast and in the audience talk about their rediscovered love for this landscape and its people, and I know just what they mean. I fall in love with this place every night all over again in being part of these performances. And it feels to me that the audiences – whether from near or far – are always in agreement.

At his memorial service earlier this morning, I heard it said that Marlin had a bit of a restless spirit, but that he had finally found a home base in the Sautee community. It became his home; the place where he married and had children and where he touched many through the roles he played on stage – the Scarecrow in "The Wizard of Oz," Don Quixote in "Man of La Mancha." He seemed to be drawn toward characters with big hearts and impossible dreams.

The current lack of rain has left us thirsty and dry, but the rivers of stories keep flowing. What would we rather know about ourselves and our neighbors – the television tales meant for shock value or the stories that reflect who we are and who we can be in community? I know which ones feel more satisfying and they're playing out right now in the historic gymnasium in Sautee.

The Taste of Summer

My typical breakfast tends to involve cereal and fruit, plus cups of strong, hot tea. I have nothing against good coffee, and sometimes enjoy a cup of decaf in the afternoon, or as an accompaniment to the eggs and toast or pancakes that I might whip up on Saturdays. And in the winter, my cold cereal is often replaced with oatmeal or cream of rice hot cereal. In general, I'm a big fan of breakfast food.

As a kid, I tended to gravitate toward the sweetened cereals that were popular at the time, such as Lucky Charms or Cap'n Crunch. In fact, I used to theorize that you could tell something about a person's ability to delay gratification based on how they ate their Lucky Charms. Did they pace themselves, always combining the oat cereal with the "marshmallow charms" in every spoonful? Did they eat all the sugary marshmallow bits first and begrudgingly eat the cereal last (if at all)? Or did they, like me, eat all the cereal first and save the sweetest part for last? Some university ought to take a look at that.

These days, my cold cereal is usually a combination of the honey nut and less sweet original-flavor versions of Cheerios. In the non-summer months, I add slices of banana and am very satisfied with that. But in the summer? Now that's another story altogether. The summer months bring sweet and juicy blueberries and fresh peaches, and all of a sudden my breakfast flavors have jumped a few serious notches. Kind of like when Emeril says "Bam!"

Back in June, I drove quite a distance to Atlantic Beach, North Carolina for a conference. It's one of those places to which there is no straight-line path on one good highway – you almost "can't get there from here." First I had to make my way over to I-85 and take that to I-26, then to I-95, and then, finally, I drove the last several hours on two-lane back roads through small towns till I arrived at the beach. It was quite a journey.

So when I passed a blueberry farm, there was no doubt in my mind that I'd be stopping there to make a purchase on the way home. A few days later, I carried a ten pound box of heavenly sweetness back to my mountain home.

At this moment, there's a huge basket of peaches filling up my kitchen with their wonderful perfume. Since there's no way I'll be able to eat all of them before they go bad, I think I'll have to start making pies and crisps, and maybe some preserves too. Or, like I did with a lot of the berries, I'll have to figure out how they can be frozen. That just might allow me to cheat a little bit and extend some of summer's sweetness into the fall.

My love of summer's flavors doesn't stop with the fruits. I've been savoring red, orange and yellow tomatoes when I can find them at the local farm markets, and I've found a source for some of the hands-down best Silver Queen white corn that I've ever eaten in my life.

Lately, it seems every day brings another news story about food that's carrying some kind of deadly disease. Often that food comes to our grocery stores from great distances away – using up a lot of expensive fuel in the process. I've read that most foods travel about 1500 miles to land on our tables! With oil and gas prices skyrocketing, it's no wonder our food prices keep going up.

So it seems to me that it's a good thing to buy locally grown food. Each bite is a celebration for my taste buds, it's good for our precious earth to burn less fuel, and it helps our neighbors when we support our local growers and markets. Now that's what I call a win-win situation.

Magic in the Pasture

Before I "saw the light" and moved to Habersham County, I used to sit in my condominium in metro Atlanta and dream of one day living in a restored old farmhouse where the land held a combination of pasture and woods and maybe even an old barn. Now, the place I call home holds exactly that combination of pleasures. In fact, when I saw the newspaper listing that advertised this house, it seemed as if it screamed out "Sheri, this is your home!"

The twenty months that I've lived in this place have offered a lot of new discoveries of many things of beauty, most of which can only be found in the kind of landscape by which I am now surrounded. I guess it's possible that tiny frogs the size of my thumbnail lived in Marietta somewhere, but I never saw them. And I never before witnessed Eastern Phoebes and the way they sit on branches and wag their tails before they fly out to snag a bug in the backyard. Nor had I ever watched multiple pairs of Indigo Buntings at a birdfeeder with their iridescent blue feathers sparkling in the sunshine.

As a child, I used to love the song "Moonshadow" by Cat Stevens, but I never knew that the moonlight could actually create the kinds of shadows that we experience all the time in the sunshine. I think that's because I never had a pasture before.

When you live where buildings are all crowded together and there's a lot of light pollution from pulsating city life there's just not enough space to allow that beautiful mother moon to paint the landscape with her light brush. But on clear nights when I walk the dog out into that field – even when there's maybe only a half moon – everything around me glows and I can see my very own moonshadow as I stroll along.

Of course, the starlight is brighter in a pasture too. When the visible sky space is wider and clearer, the stars hang like garlands of diamonds as they twinkle their greetings sent many light years ago.

But there's another kind of light in the pasture that is probably the most magical of all, and it's only seen on summer nights. That's when the fireflies pop like bubbles from a champagne glass everywhere I look. Oh, I'm used to lightening bugs. I spent many an evening in my youth catching them in jars and never tired of that mysterious luminescence. But once again the expanse of the pasture just means I can see a whole lot more of them at one time than I'd ever seen before.

I find this to be proof, once again, of God's flamboyant grace and over-the-top joy in what is beautiful. Sometimes I'll just stand there and watch the flow of sparkles as they explode in solos and in symphonies for the eyes. And it makes me laugh and smile.

One of our county commissioners recently commented that there was not a pasture in a certain area that would not eventually become a subdivision. Though I understand that people moving in need homes – just like I did – and that people with land like to turn a profit, it makes me shudder to think that without proper planning for what needs protecting we'll blink our eyes and the day will come when everything that's precious about this place will be paved over.

If there are no more pastures, how will our children see their own moonshadows? Where will they get the chance to see a hundred fireflies blinking in one place? Holy light is not just found in church – we can find it right here in the pasture.

Cats and Dogs

Despite Bill Murray's rant in the movie "Caddyshack" about "cats and dogs sleeping together!" as a sign of the end of the world, I'm wondering these days about how cats and dogs actually do get along. Growing up, we had a dog named Cuddles and always two cats at a time, but I don't remember a lot about their specific relationships (other than that whichever cat was older would always swat at the younger).

Thirteen years ago I adopted two female kittens from the same litter and named them Carly and Phoebe (after women singers of the 1970s). Because they've always been indoor cats with limited social contacts, they've had no exposure to any other animals, feline or otherwise.

So when I adopted my dog Cotton a little over a year ago, Carly and Phoebe were not pleased. They looked at me as if I had insanely brought some kind of beast into the house and alternated between hiding and hissing. Fifteen months together have brought a kind of tolerable co-existence, but I would not call them friends. Though there are times when I think Phoebe's protesting is more for show than for real.

While at a lecture the other day, the church bishop commented that one of the differences between "red" and "blue" states in this country is that the blue states tend to be along either the West or East Coast of the United States, and that people who live in those seaboard areas are regularly exposed to folks from all different kinds of backgrounds. Meaning blue state residents have no other choice but to broaden their worldview a little to allow for the differences in race, culture and religion that they see around them every day. On the other hand, red state areas can tend to hold concentrations of people that are more alike.

I think there's some truth to that. When I hit the first grade in my small neighborhood school, the best friend that I met there was a Jewish boy who lived a couple of blocks away from me. We walked together to school and back every day through the eighth grade, until he moved to a far-away state. In fact, he was not the only Jewish friend I knew, and I attended more than one service in a synagogue in those years. Though the paths of our lives unfolded in many different directions, they intersected again a while back when Stephen and his family moved to Atlanta. We are still dear friends.

And why shouldn't I feel a kinship with Jewish friends? Jesus was, after all, a Jew. Judaism gave birth to Christianity so it seems to me that for a Christian to disrespect Jewish folks is akin to disrespecting your mother.

But I have hope that we can all learn to get along with each other. Late last winter, I adopted a young male cat who'd been left behind when his owner moved away. Cotton and I would pass by that house nearly every morning on our walks, so we met Tangy when he was just a baby. He'd spend his days hanging out in the backyard with his own dogs, and they were clearly good buddies.

So when we passed the house several days after the owner and her dogs had left and Tangy came rushing out to meet us, rubbing up against Cotton like they were long lost pals, I knew I had to bring him home with us. An hour after arriving on my porch, Tangy made it clear that he was happy to be our newest family member.

Every day he stares up at Cotton's face with absolute adoration, reaching up with his paws to ask for kisses. And Cotton obliges like a devoted big brother. Somehow, I can't interpret this "cats and dogs playing together" as the end of the world. Maybe it's just the beginning of a new and welcome kind of world.

Picking Blueberries

Belarus is not a country that I've ever visited or even know a lot about. But I recently made a small contribution to the welfare of orphans in that country by picking blueberries at Sydney Roland's farm.

I've expressed often my love of fresh summer fruit and the particular fondness I have for blueberries in my morning breakfast. So when I heard that Mr. Roland had opened up his blueberries for the picking and that the $4 per gallon charge would be donated to that good cause, I decided to drive over there.

I parked my car and grabbed a bucket. It was a warm Sunday afternoon and with few people around I was mostly alone as I wove in and out of the bushes looking for clumps of plump fruit.

I'm not sure if the berries had already been descended upon by hungry people or flocks of birds, but it seemed the pickings were a little slim at first. I knew better than to think that there would be gallons of berries for the taking within immediate easy reach, but I wasn't sure what to expect. I've not done a lot of berry picking in my life.

Because I didn't grow up on a farm, I've not been a direct participant in the steps between stem and table. The sweat and muscle it takes to get the bounty to my plate have been paid for with my cash without being witnessed with my eyes or with my own labor.

After a bit of wandering, I finally found a spot where there seemed to be enough berries to gather. I stood there in the heat of the day reaching deep within the branches and smiling when my fingers were able to surround and release a few berries from their grip. There began to be a rhythm to what I was doing that was choreographed with a soundtrack of bugs and birdsong, making the task easier. And as I tried to keep my feet away from fire ant mounds and snakes, I caught sight of a skink or two.

I learned that the berries were never on the fringes of the bushes. At first, I kept trying to reach in with a good stretch so that I could keep my body from getting scraped, but eventually I allowed myself to move deeper and deeper into the bushes themselves. There were times when I almost could not tell where the branches ended and my body began.

Every now and then I'd get wrapped up in some thorny places and have a hard time getting out again. And isn't that a lot like life in general? It just seems to be the nature of things that what is good and sweet also brings its share of thorns. We can shake our fist and complain all we want, but it still won't change the fact that this world is a mixture of darkness and light, of pleasure and pain, of good and bad.

Once we leave this world, it's my belief that we'll enter a state where there is only love and light; a place where suffering ends. But as long as we are wearing the skin suits of earthbound life, we'll experience both joy and suffering.

It took me ninety minutes to pick about three-quarters of a bucket of blueberries. I came away from that experience with a greater appreciation for the farmers who grow our food, and the people – usually immigrants – who are willing to pick it on my behalf. And though the slight scratches on my skin are nothing compared to the wounds on those Belarus orphans' hearts, I'm hoping that my meager offering of money for blueberries helps to ease their suffering even just a little bit.

Watch the Signs

In times of great change and upheaval, whether in one's personal life or in the life of the country we live in, it's easy to get discouraged. Sometimes the pressures we face seem absolutely unmanageable and in those moments we can feel powerless and paralyzed with no clarity on what to do next.

When I left my last full time "day job" with a software company in Atlanta, it was the last in a long line of "downsizings" that are so common in Corporate America today. If I added up all the times I was "moved on" when it wasn't my choice – due to company ownership changes or any number of reasons out of my control – I think there were six times in fifteen years that I was left without work.

With my first job loss, I was devastated and felt like my world had come to an end. But after the third or fourth experience, I began to realize the truth of that old saying that "whenever God closes a door, He opens a window."

I think one of the things that keep us stuck is that we often limit our vision for new opportunities to the doors that look like the same old door that just slammed shut, completely missing the windows that are sliding open to the left and right of us. In order to be led through the new window, we have to be willing to watch where the life is sprouting and move in that direction, not keep banging our heads against doorways that are dead.

I remember hearing a lecture by a popular author several years ago who spoke of a man whose life was falling apart – job loss, divorce, etc. – and how he said that he knew God must be behind all of this turmoil because who else could turn up the heat on every burner at the same time? I call those periods "fire times" because in those moments it feels as if everything we know is being burned away.

God is turning up the heat in my own life again. Since the last time I was given that "pink slip" and shown the company exit, I've been doing my best to earn my living as an artist. I've been booking performances and speaking engagements, selling music CDs, working with high school students on creative writing, but even after five years, the disappointing truth is that I've not been able to adequately support myself. And since there's no one else in the wings helping to pay my bills, I thought maybe I should be watching for signs of new windows.

For two years or more, I've been praying to be led to the work I was born to do even if that was not based in music. More recently, Randy Pausch's "Last Lecture" moved me to want to be doing more to help others achieve their dreams.

One path I've considered for many years is to go to seminary but, for various reasons, I just couldn't see myself in parish ministry. A few weeks ago, a series of meaningful coincidences whacked me upside the head and showed me a new vision – a completely new window. This window-path goes from seminary to a career in teaching and writing, so I'm now exploring several divinity schools to begin a masters program next Fall. I will be sad to leave my mountain home, but I feel no doubt that God is calling me in this direction.

Yet it is very stressful to imagine such an enormous undertaking, and the decisions and questions have been overwhelming. For days now I've felt stuck and afraid. But here's one of the signs I've seen – for the last four days a praying mantis has been sitting on the window of my office. Her posture is a perfect reminder that it's okay to be still, to listen, to pray and to trust that I am not alone. Not now. Not ever.

Morning Light

Finding Home

Growing up in a church that followed the lectionary tradition meant that I heard most all the stories from Scripture. And one of my favorites has always been the one about the Prodigal Son.

One day several years ago, I was waiting in the church library to meet with a friend and came across Henri Nouwen's book "The Return of the Prodigal Son: A Story of Homecoming." As the minutes ticked away, I stood and turned and turned the pages, descending deeper and deeper into the text. When my friend arrived, I checked out the book and took it with me on a trip that weekend to a retreat house in Dublin, Georgia called the Green Bough House of Prayer. In that sweet space of silence and tender care, I felt myself falling in love with the story even more completely.

Nouwen's journey into this story came after he encountered Rembrandt's painting of the parable on a poster in the office of a coworker. In the book, he writes: "Rembrandt's embrace [of the father and son] remained imprinted on my soul far more profoundly than any temporary expression of emotional support. It had brought me into touch with something within me that lies far beyond the ups and downs of a busy life, something that represents the ongoing yearning of the human spirit, the yearning for a final return, an unambiguous sense of safety, a lasting home."

In how many places have I looked for home? How many jobs have I tried to turn into the place where I belonged? How many relationships? My restless spirit has alighted on branch after branch, seeking to finally find one place where I could remain a while and feel safe. Surely, it seemed, I would eventually carve out a groove for myself where I would no longer feel like Life's Outsider?

For almost two years now, I've lived in a place of inspiring beauty that has poured great nourishment into my soul and heart. I have felt more connected to this ground than to any other on which my feet have walked. I've been welcomed by people in a community that I've loved and imagined that I might live here in the Appalachian foothills of northeast Georgia the rest of my days.

But once again God is calling me to step out into unknown territory – to a new type of soil where I can plant myself with roots that seek deeper knowledge of God and greater understanding of my Christian tradition. And I have hopes that this planting will allow me to reach out one day toward students with branches and fluttering leaves that will inspire and lift them.

So what about home? And in all my time spent searching for home "out there" what have I actually been leaving? Nouwen describes this prodigal-seeking as a "denial of the spiritual reality that I belong to God with every part of my being, that God holds me safe in an eternal embrace, that I am indeed carved in the palms of God's hands and hidden in their shadows... Leaving home is living as though I do not yet have a home and must look far and wide to find one." He answers the question with this wisdom: "Home is the center of my being where I can hear the voice that says: 'You are my Beloved, on you my favor rests.' "

Once the process of seminary applications have been completed, an admission is granted and scholarship funds are identified, I'll be packing up my things and my four-legged, furry family and heading to a new place to live. And I will make that place my physical home. But I will carry my spiritual Home within me, in the voice that whispers light into every darkness.

Acknowledgements

I would like to express my deepest gratitude to all of those who encouraged me in my writing and who opened doors for me so that I might share my ideas with readers. First, I want to acknowledge Rob Moore, editor of *The Northeast Georgian* newspaper in Habersham County, Georgia who gave a songwriter who was new to his small, rural community a chance to write and be published based on little more than an idea. I'd also like to thank Treva Bennett, copy editor for the paper, who received my columns with a kind spirit.

I want to offer my fondest and warmest love to Mrs. Verna Brown who asked Rob to let me know that she loved my columns and wanted to meet me. What has blossomed since then is a sweet friendship that I will always treasure.

I am thankful to Georgia Public Broadcasting for airing some of my writing in commentary form, allowing my voice to grace the airwaves throughout the state of Georgia. And I am grateful to all the audience members I have met along the way who welcomed me into their churches, theatres and community centers to share my songs and stories. I've been blessed by their positive spirit, financial support and their listening ears.

I have been graced with several loving mentors who have guided me over these recent years in so many ways as I've done my best to navigate both stormy and calmer seas – Rev. Lynnsay Buehler, Jerry Wright and Joyce Rockwood Hudson. There are not enough words to express my most heartfelt appreciation for what you have all done for me.

I am grateful to the members and staff of the Lutheran Church of the Resurrection in Marietta and of Nacoochee Presbyterian Church in Sautee who have provided me spiritual home bases.

Finally, I am thankful for the family members and friends who have walked with me lo these many years in faith and love.

.

Printed in the United States
139344LV00001B/22/P

9 781935 028055